Mary Gorman

Caiques

Everything About Health, Behavior, Feeding, and Care

Filled with Full-color Photographs
Illustrations by Michele Earle-Bridges

2 CONTENTS

IS A CAIQUE FOR YOU?

One of the first things you should know about caiques is how to pronounce their name. The first syllable begins with a k sound and rhymes with the word my; the second syllable is stressed and pronounced "EEK": "Ky-EEK."

The Unique Caique

"Watching a caique at play is a little like watching a hyperactive child who hasn't taken his medication yet," a breeder of caiques once told me. That's not a bad analogy—caique parrots are one of the most energetic and enthusiastically playful parrots on the planet, literally hopping from one adventure to the next as they explore, manipulate, and play with everything that they have the pleasure to encounter.

Caiques are a genus of small (approximately 9–9½ inches, or 23–25 cm, long) parrots from South America. They are native to the northern portions of South America, where they live in flocks in the canopies of the rain forest. They travel in pairs or small groups and are reportedly playful even in the wild, body surfing on the broad, wet leaves of the highest trees.

Caiques are lively, curious, and always ready for adventure.

Although they have long been kept as pets by the natives of South America, they are somewhat difficult to breed in captivity and so are not as common or as well known as pets in other parts of the world.

Caiques are the only white-bellied parrots in the world. This white belly is present in both species of caique, although only one of them, the white-bellied caique, takes its name from that feature. The other species of caique is called the black-headed caique because of the cap of black feathers on the top of its head. White bellies are also sometimes referred to as yellow-thighed caiques, a name that may be more specific, but is less commonly used.

As pets, caiques are charming and extremely entertaining, but they are not what you would consider low-maintenance pets. They are not the kind of bird that can be left in a small cage and fed once a day but ignored the rest of the time. They require a large assortment of toys, a

Caiques may be small, but they like to play and roughhouse.

on their backs to play. Baby caiques will lie on their backs so that their clutch mates can wrestle with them, jumping on top and grabbing at each other with their feet. Adult caiques frequently let their owners carry them lying on their backs in the palm of their hands. One caique I know of even enjoys letting its owner place it on its back on the kitchen table and spin it like a top, resulting in squeals of apparent delight from the bird.

Young caiques sometimes actually fall asleep lying on their backs on the cage floor. Many an unknowing caique owner has gone to the bird's cage and had a terrible fright when he or she finds his or her beloved pet lying on its back on the floor of its cage with its eyes closed.

Caiques are also champion hoppers, jumping up and down on both feet like a demented wind-up toy. Some caiques will hop when music is played, making it seem like they are dancing to the sound. It usually takes very little encouragement from owners to get their caique hopping, often to the delight of guests.

Caiques are much more physical than many other species of parrot, and enjoy snuggling and rubbing up against their owners—particularly rubbing their bodies against their owners' hair.

Caique owners need to be very clear in their expectations and the limits that they impose upon their birds, because a caique that gets overly excited while playing can be very difficult to calm down. A caique is not always an easy pet, but most people find that the payoff in terms of the years of joy and affection their pets bring is worth the effort.

varied diet, and a considerable amount of human interaction and supervision. They are enthusiastic chewers and seemingly fearless as they explore their environment. Like all pet birds, they should have an annual veterinary exam to guarantee that they remain in good health. Although they are diminutive in size, they require a much larger cage than other birds their size to accommodate their high energy level and the number of toys they require to keep them amused and occupied.

The payoff for those who are willing to invest the time and equipment that caiques require is a charming, intelligent, and thoroughly entertaining pet. Caiques may be small, but they like to play and roughhouse. They are one of the few parrots that seem to enjoy lying

A black-headed caique explores its toys. Caiques are active, inquisitive, and curious.

Is a Caique the Right Pet for You?

For some people, the question of whether or not to get a caique is moot—you may have already acquired a caique and are simply looking for information to provide your new pet with the best possible care. Others may be wisely reading this book as research to find the species of bird that is the best fit for their tastes and lifestyle. This chapter is intended for them.

There are many reasons that people may want to share their homes with a pet caique—and just as many reasons not to. Parrots are one of the worst impulse buys that a person can make, and with a potential life span of up to 40 years, the consequences of a wrong decision can be very long lasting indeed.

Parrots are very demanding pets. The idea that parrots are easy to care for, need to be fed only once a day, and can otherwise be ignored is absolutely wrong. Parrots are intelligent birds who need a high level of attention and inter-action. A parrot that is placed in a cage and essentially ignored is liable to develop behavior problems, which can include biting, screaming, pulling out its own feathers or, in extreme cases, picking at its skin until it bleeds. It is easier—and kinder—not to bring a caique into your home at all than to bring one into a less-than-ideal situation.

Parrots are also not for those who are com-pulsively neat. Discarded shells and husks, molted feathers, dander, and bits of chewed-up wooden toys may all make their way out of the cage and onto the surrounding floor and furni-ture. Food and water dishes need to be cleaned daily, if not more often.

A caique outside its cage needs constant supervision. They are extremely curious and without any sense of the potential hazards in your household. Caiques are also particularly aggressive when it comes to chewing wood—your wooden household furnishings will be fair game in their eyes.

The noise factor is a relative concern. Caiques are not silent, but in terms of sheer potential volume, they are not the noisiest of parrots, either. Some people consider their caiques to be fairly noisy, whereas others don't. And like people, some individuals will be noisier than others. Observing a caique before you buy it may be the best way to gauge whether the sounds it makes fall within your comfort level, although this isn't absolutely foolproof. Many caiques seem to adjust their noise level to that

Caiques are one of the few parrots that enjoy lying on their backs. More than one caique owner has been frightened to find their new baby bird lying on its back on the bottom of the cage, only to find that the bird is merely sleeping.

of the household—if you have noisy kids or barking dogs, the caique will try to make itself louder, simply to be heard.

Although caiques themselves are small, they require a cage that would accommodate a much larger bird. If you are considering a caique because you have limited available space in your home, you would do better to consider a different kind of bird. They do not do well in small cages.

Caiques are not as easily bred in captivity as some other birds, and that is reflected in their their cost. In addition to the initial cost of the bird will be the cost of the cage, toys, supplies, food, and veterinary care. Owning a caique is not cheap.

They also need daily time out of their cages, a supply of toys to play with, and a lot of human interaction. They need to have clear boundaries set in terms of their behavior and what is allowed. A well-socialized caique is a joy; a caique who has no understanding of what is acceptable and what is not is a terror.

Caiques are not good pets for children. Small beaks may still cause great pain, and bites are likely if the bird is startled or handled roughly. And given their long potential lifespan, caiques are likely to outlive the child's interest. Even the most devoted child will probably have to leave the bird behind when he or she goes off to college, leaving Mom and Dad to take care of the bird—a responsibility they may not particularly want.

Caiques may or may not get along well with another bird in the house, but they should never be allowed unsupervised around other household pets, such as dogs, cats, and ferrets. Even a very docile dog may snap at a caique that approaches it, jumping up and down in front of it and wanting to play. Cats pose a special problem because their saliva contains a bacteria called pasteurella that is toxic to parrots. Your caique may initially survive an encounter with a cat, but if its teeth broke the skin, the caique could still die of the infection in a matter of hours unless antibiotics are administered. Ferrets will also view your caique

Facts to Consider

Pro	Con
Highly interactive pet	Require a lot of interactive time
Long life span	Expensive
Capable of talking	Require a lot of cage space
Moderate noise level	Messy
Extremely entertaining	Enthusiastic chewers of wood
	Need clear behavioral limits set

as prey and aggressively stalk it. You can keep a caique as a pet if you also own these other animals, but you'll need to be extra vigilant to ensure its safety.

However, caiques *do* make excellent pets for people who are well informed, willing to pay the expenses that owning an exotic bird entails, and have enough time to interact properly with their pets. They are bright, attractive, and endlessly entertaining.

Caiques tend to be good whistlers but are not known to be outstanding talkers. Many manage to learn to say a few words, but they are not as clear or as talkative as many other species of birds. A typical caique will learn to say only a few words or phrases throughout its lifetime, although there are exceptions. You may come across an individual who is a prodigious talker, or one who never speaks at all. Although caiques are capable of talking, there is no guarantee that a particular individual will talk. So if you have your heart set on a bird that is likely to talk, a caique may not be the best choice.

One advantage that a caique has over other kinds of birds is that they are very interested in people. They enjoy interacting and seem to be particularly happy if they have an audience.

And because of their playful nature, they will enjoy exploring your pockets, climbing up the inside of your shirt, and gently wrestling with your fingers.

Caiques do not make good pets for children. Even older children who are mature enough to be responsible will probably have to leave the birds behind when they go off to college.

A caique can be kept with another parrot. The white-bellied caique in this photo is preening a bronze-wing pionus. However, they should be carefully supervised when they are together, particularly in the beginning.

Caiques can sometimes be taught to do simple tricks. They don't seem to be intimidated by the presence of strangers and aren't likely to freeze up if you have company. The introduction of a second caique does not seem to negatively affect the owner-pet relationship; if you and your bird have an affectionate relationship, you should be able to maintain that in spite of the new addition.

With proper medical care and increasingly better nutrition, caiques are living longer than ever before, and it's likely that their potential life span may increase as more becomes known about their health and optimum diet. This long life span is a definite advantage over dogs and cats and smaller birds such as canaries, budgies, and cockatiels.

In the end, it's up to you to weigh the pros and cons. You're the only one who can decide whether or not a caique is the right bird for you.

The Species

As mentioned before, there are two different species of caique—the white-bellied and the black-headed. Although there is really no difference in terms of pet potential, white bellies tend to be more difficult in captivity and thus

The potential life span of a caique is approximately 40 years, so make sure you're ready for a long-term commitment.

tend to be a little more expensive than their black-headed counterparts.

As is the case with many parrots, both white-bellied and black-headed caiques have sub-species. A subspecies is recognized when scientists determine that there is a slight differ-ence between the birds found in one location and the birds found in another. These differ-ences are very small and don't affect the type of pet the caique will be. The different subspecies are listed here purely for informational purposes.

Caiques can be one of the most entertaining pets you'll ever own.

There's not much difference in pet potential between white-bellied caiques (left) and black-headed caiques (right). Both can make charming, interactive pets.

Black-headed Caique Species and Subspecies

Black-headed Caique

Scientific name: Pionites melanocephala melanocephala

Common species name: black-headed caique

First scientific record: Carrolis Linnaeus in 1758

Description: This is the nominate species of the black-headed caique. The black-headed caique has a green back, wings, and rump with a creamy white chest and abdomen. The top half of the head is black and the lower half of the head is orange-yellow, which has the effect of looking like the bird is wearing a Zorro-type mask, and a thin horizontal green stripe marks the area between the black and yellow areas of the head. The thighs and flanks are the same color as the lower half of the head. Black-headed caiques have reddish-orange eyes with a light gray ring of skin surrounding them. Their beaks and feet are a powdery gray color with the tip of the upper beak darkening to near-black. Young black-headed caiques are somewhat paler than adults and may have some yellow amidst the white on their bellies and chest, with brown eyes and blackish bills.

Range: Southeastern Colombia, northern Brazil, northeast and southern Venezuela, French Guiana, Guyana, and Surinam

Pallid Caique

Scientific name: Pionites melanocephala pallida

First scientific record: Hans Hermann Berlepsch in 1889

Description: This subspecies is identical to the nominate species except for the fact that the normally orange-yellow throat, neck, and thighs are pure yellow and the breast and abdomen are a paler shade of white.

Range: Eastern Ecuador, south and northeastern Peru, and southern Colombia

White-bellied Caique Subspecies

Yellow-thighed Caique

Scientific name: Pionites leucogaster xanthomeria

First scientific record: Philip Lutley Sclater in 1857

Description: The plumage on the belly and chest is pure white. The top of the head from the nares to the back of the neck is orange-yellow. The throat, sides of the head and body, and thighs are all bright yellow. The lower back and upper-tail coverts are green interspersed with yellow. The back and wings are bright green. The eyes are reddish orange, surrounded by a whitish ring of skin. The beak is horn colored, and the feet are gray. Young white-bellied caiques have brown eyes instead of

orange ones, and the tops and backs of their heads have a smattering of black feathers mixed in among the orange-yellow, although these should molt out as the bird ages.

Because the territories of all black-headed and white-bellied caiques overlap, some scientists theorize that the yellow-thighed caique may, in fact be a hybrid of the two species.

Range: Northwestern Brazil, Ecuador, Peru, and Bolivia

Yellow-tailed Caique

Scientific name: Pionites leucogaster xanthurus

First scientific record: Walter Todd in 1925

Description: Resembles the green-thighed caique but is slightly paler. The thighs, sides, under-tail coverts, and both the upper and under sides of the tail are yellow, and the lower back and upper-tail coverts are green interspersed with yellow.

Range: Northwestern Brazil

Green-thighed Caique

Scientific name: Pionites leucogaster leucogaster

Common species name: Green-thighed caique

First scientific record: Heinrich Kuhl in 1820

Description: The plumage on the belly and chest is pure white. The top of the head from the nares to the back of the neck is orange-yellow. The sides of the head, the throat, and the under-tail coverts are bright yellow. The back, wings, thighs, and upper side of the tail are bright green. The underside of the tail is blackish green. The eyes are reddish orange, surrounded by a whitish ring of skin. The beak is horn colored and the feet are gray.

Range: Northern Brazil

GETTING READY

Once you make the decision to include a caique in your family, you can make the transition easier by getting everything ready in advance. Even though your impulse will be to bring your new pet home as soon as possible, it's better to bring it home to a waiting cage rather than get home and discover that you are not quite ready for it. This chapter will help you to know what you need to do to get ready for your pet.

Before You Bring Your Bird Home

Everyone wants to make a good first impression. You are no different. This is why you should get everything ready before you actually bring your bird home. You'll want to be able to get your bird out of its carrier and into its cage as soon as you can after you bring it home, rather than having to make it sit in that small space while you hurriedly set up the cage.

One of the first things I recommend doing once you've found your bird is to put a deposit on it, then go home and start looking for an avian veterinarian. If you buy your bird locally, whoever you purchase the bird from may be

The black feathers on the head of this white-bellied caique will disappear as it gets older.

able to recommend an avian veterinarian. Try to schedule a "new-bird" exam as soon as possible after you purchase it. With any health issue, the sooner it's discovered, the more likely it is to have a positive resolution.

I always try to schedule a visit to the veterinarian's as soon as I know when the bird is going to be coming home. If I can, I set up the appointment so that I bring the bird to the veterinarian's on the way home from the store. If a bird has been shipped by plane, I'll try to time it so that we stop at the veterinarian's office on the way home from the airport rather than stressing the bird out twice, once with the trip home and then again with the trip to the veterinarian.

Bringing your caique to the veterinarian before you bring it home may allow you to discover a problem before you become too attached to the bird. This is helpful if the bird

As far as a caique is concerned, you can never have too big a cage or too many toys.

helpful generalization isn't that far off the mark when you consider that most people buy one cage when they first get their bird, and that becomes the bird's primary home for the rest of its life.

Logic may seem to dictate that a small bird can get by with a small cage, but that's not true with a caique. Caiques are happiest when they're in motion, and consequently, they need a lot of room to move around. Add to that the necessity of a large selection of toys, and your caique is going to take up much more space than you'd expect for a small bird.

A minimum cage size is approximately 24 inches × 36 inches × 24 inches (60 cm × 91 cm × 60 cm), but the larger the better. You might want to consider a cage on wheels so that you can move it more easily for vacuuming under and around it.

The cage bars should be no more than ¾ of an inch (2 cm) apart—any farther than that and you'll run the risk of the bird being able to get its head caught between the bars, resulting in injury or death.

Secondhand or antique cages should be viewed with caution. Not only are they unlikely to be suitable because of the size and bar spacing, but in the past, cages were frequently made with metals such as lead or zinc—substances we now know to be toxic to birds. Even if the bars themselves are made with a harmless metal, they may have been soldered together with lead or zinc. Caiques, being inherently curious, are likely to try to taste these metals, resulting in irreversible brain damage or even death. No matter how attrac-

has a condition that will require you to return it to the seller. If you have other birds at home, the prompt checkup may also keep them from being exposed to any potentially contagious conditions that the new caique may have.

Don't try to cut corners by skipping the veterinarian's visit. Even if your bird is healthy, being able to examine it now will help your veterinarian know what is normal for your caique (weight, chemical levels, etc.) and give him or her something to compare with should the bird ever become sick in the future.

The Cage

The stock answer to the question "How big a cage should I buy for my caique?" is "The biggest one you can afford." This not-very-

tive an antique cage might be, it's not worth risking the life of your bird.

Some newer models of cages come with a play top—a series of perches, ladders, and swings built into the roof of the cage. These can be great fun for your caique, but be careful not to buy one where the height of the play top will put the bird higher than your eye level. One theory says that a bird that can look down on its owner is more likely to develop behavioral issues. Whether you buy into that theory or not, your bird will be easier to retrieve and more visible—thus easier to enjoy—if you don't have to look up to see it.

The exact color and model of cage you choose is a matter of personal taste. If you want a cage to be a particular color to match your décor, then by all means, look for a cage that color. I recommend that you buy a cage with a small door above each dish as well as a larger opening that you can use to reach your whole arm into the cage. The small doors are very convenient for when you need to service the food dishes but don't want to have to open the cage up wide and risk letting the bird out. Some caiques have a penchant for getting out of their cage when you are already running late for work and really can't afford to spend the time chasing them to put them back inside.

Whether you want a cage with a rounded top or a flat top is also purely a matter of personal taste. It has been suggested, however, that parrots are more comfortable in a cage with corners than in a circular cage both because they like to be able to retreat into a corner and because they find the curving walls somewhat disorienting. You should also try to find a cage that is wider than it is tall. Birds fly horizontally, not vertically, so a wide cage

allows them more space to exercise than a tall one does. For the reasons mentioned previously, try to find a cage whose top is lower than your eye level. Also avoid cages with walls that taper outward as they get higher, or that have sections that extend beyond the base of the cage. You want to make sure that any droppings end up inside the cage rather than on your carpet.

Many cages now come with "skirts"—metal edging that extends beyond the cage's outside perimeter to catch any bits of shell, husks, or other debris that may fall outside the cage. These will slightly increase the amount of area your cage takes up, but will also cut down on the mess that reaches the floor.

The easiest way to line the bottom of the cage is with ordinary newspapers. Some pet stores and supply catalogs may offer cage-lining papers, some of which may have grit attached. These are not necessary. Wood shavings and corncob bedding may be sold to line the cage

Caiques, like this young white-bellied, enjoy exploring tight spaces.

floor, but will become scattered outside the cage as the bird flaps and plays. Even worse, these pose a special hazard because they may retain moisture and harbor mold, which can cause respiratory problems in caiques.

One of the easiest ways to keep the cage clean is to slit the seams of the newspapers you use to line the bottom. Simply remove the top sheet of newspaper every day until you go through all the layers, at which point you can lay a new batch of newspapers on the cage floor.

Location

Selecting the proper location for your caique's cage is important, especially at first. The caique needs to be close enough to observe the family, yet removed enough from the center of activity for it to feel safe during the adjustment period. Kitchens are not a good choice because of the risk of toxic fumes being given off by overheated nonstick coating on pans and self-cleaning ovens. (See "In the Kitchen" in the section on safety.)

The cage needs to be at least one caique body length, plus 6 inches (15 cm) away from all surrounding objects. If the beak can reach it, the caique will chew it. This includes not just furniture, but draperies, sills, and woodwork.

For the comfort of the bird, the cage should be in an area free from drafts. Most caiques enjoy being able to look out a window, but you don't want to have the bird in unrelenting direct sunlight or in a room that is uncomfortably hot. Use your own comfort level as a guide. If you would be comfortable in a particular spot without feeling too hot or too cold, then it's probably all right for your caique.

Avoid keeping your bird in a room with a sliding glass door. I prefer to keep my birds in the upstairs of my house rather than in a room that opens directly to the outside. Even though my birds are clipped, there are always children running in and out of my house during the summer months, and it would take only one careless moment for a startled bird whose wings were just on the verge of growing out again to fly out through the door.

If you own other birds already, you should not put the new bird in the same room with them until you have had the new bird checked by a veterinarian and waited for a 30-day quarantine period. Once quarantine is up, make sure that the cages are placed far enough apart that the bird in one cage cannot reach the toes of the bird in the second cage as it clings to the inside of its cage. Once your caique has had a chance to settle and become used to its new home and its residents, you will probably want to move the cage closer to the center of household activity. Caiques love to watch household activities and to be talked to and admired by their human family. Family rooms or dens where the bird can have a lot of human observation and interaction are ideal locations for a sociable caique.

Caiques who were raised together or who shared a cage at their place of purchase can be housed in a single cage. When introducing a new caique, however, it's best to keep it in a separate cage, at least during its period of adjustment, because the resident bird may feel very protective of its "territory." It is best to keep the new bird's cage across the room from the resident bird's, gradually moving both cages closer together over the course of several days. If you see the birds willingly sharing a cage, then it's probably safe to let them be housed together, although you should be on the lookout for signs of aggression, particularly over the course of the first few days.

Perches

It used to be that every bird cage came with the same kind of perch—a wooden dowel with a uniform diameter. These are still standard issue for most cages, but they are far from the only or the best option now.

Perches come in a variety of materials: milled wood, natural branches, plastic or PVC piping, cloth, rope, clay, and even concrete. No one perching material can be unequivocally declared to be better than the others, but each has its own particular benefits and drawbacks.

The traditional wooden dowel works well, which is why it's been used for perches for so many years. These dowels, however, are no match for a bird who likes to chew, and caiques are champion chewers. With a caique, odds are that the wood will eventually be chewed through. This takes a while, but eventually these wooden perches will need to be replaced.

A bigger concern with wooden dowels is that they maintain the same diameter all the way across. Because of this, the bird's foot is always in the same position whenever it perches, unlike in the wild, where they can perch on different widths of tree branches. This is not a healthy arrangement and may become uncomfortable for the bird.

Wooden dowel perches are available now that are like spindles, with varying widths across the length of the perch. These are still subject to being chewed, but allow for better foot health because the bird's feet have to adjust to the contours of the perch.

Another alternative to the wooden dowel perch is a manzanita branch. Manzanita is a

Never buy a baby bird that isn't fully feathered; always look for a fully weaned bird instead.

small tree or shrub from the southwestern United States that has exceptionally hard wood. Manzanita branches are made into perches by drilling a bolt into the cut end of a branch and using that bolt to fasten the branch to the side of the cage with a washer and a wing nut. Although it's not 100 percent chew resistant, it will certainly slow down even the most industrious caique beak. Manzanita perches are more expensive than ordinary wood, but they have the added benefit of being branches rather than dowels, and thus have a natural shape and are better for your bird's feet.

Perches made of a heavy plastic or PVC piping offer the most sanitary option for perches because their uniform surface makes them easy to wipe clean and to disinfect. Like wooden dowels, however, their consistent diameter makes them less healthy for your bird's feet.

A well-stocked pet supply store may offer an almost-overwhelming variety of choices. It may take some trial and error to find out which products you and your bird prefer.

Their smooth surface may also make them more slippery than perches made of other materials, which would be a concern particularly if you had a caique with missing toes, nails, or other foot problems.

Cloth or cotton rope perches have the advantage of being gentler on the feet and may be machine washable. Perches made of thick braids of cloth strips wrapped around a flexible wire are convenient because they can be bent into a variety of shapes, even bent into an angle rather than having to reach straight across from one side of the cage to the other. This can be a wonderful advantage when you are trying to fit a variety of hanging toys inside the cage. It also allows more options when you want to rearrange the cage's furnishings. The downside of these perches is that after a while the repeated stress of the bird's nails on the fiber can cause the materials to fray. This raises the possibility of the caique's nails getting tangled up in the fraying perch, possibly resulting in injury to the bird. If you use one of these perches, inspect it occasionally for fraying, and if you notice that the material is starting to fray, replace the perch.

Clay perches are generally made with clay that comes from the cliffs of South America. These cliffs are a great tourist attraction because of the large numbers of parrots who gather on them daily to eat the clay found there. The exact reason that caiques eat clay isn't known for certain. It's believed that eating this clay either provides them with minerals that are necessary to their diets or helps to settle their stomachs after they eat acidic fruits. If you decide to provide a perch made of South American clay (they are often sold as "Manu clay perches," after the Manu River cliffs in Brazil), its irregular shape will provide a varied grip for your bird's feet, thus improving its health. A diligent caique will probably manage to chew off small bits of the perch, but it is non-toxic and may be swallowed.

Concrete perches are marketed as being useful in keeping parrots' toenails dull. They also generally have a slightly tapered shape that allows the bird to move its feet into different positions as it perches. The drawback is that the concrete can be irritating to the bottoms of the bird's feet. If you opt to use a concrete

This happy caique has a selection of toys to choose from to keep him busy.

perch and notice that your caique is favoring one foot or that its feet seem to be tender, you might want to remove the perch for a while and replace it with one made of a different material to see if that brings any relief.

If you live in an area that you know is free from pesticides and herbicides, you may also want to use a natural branch as a perch. Trees such as maple, pine, apple, and birch are all safe for your bird to chew on, and their branches can make suitable perches for your caique. If you choose to use a natural branch as a perch for your bird, remove all the leaves and wash the branch thoroughly with soap and hot water. You should then place the branch in the oven and bake it at 250°F for approximately 15 minutes to kill any insects or their larva that may be lurking beneath the bark. The branch can then be arranged in the cage by propping it against or between the cage bars. Natural branches make interesting perches for your bird, but are also subject to chewing and will need to be replaced more often than a store-bought, more chew-resistant perch. Because of this, you may want to gather and prepare several branches at a time and save the extra to replace the branches in the cage as they are chewed to bits.

Each of these types of materials has its pros and cons, but the best thing to do is offer your bird a variety of perches made of different materials so that it can choose which it prefers. My own experience is that parrots tend to prefer the highest perch in the cage, presumably because they feel safer being up high. If you notice that your bird has a preference, you might want to try moving that perch to the highest spot in the cage so that the bird will feel both secure and comfortable.

Dishes

Most cages come with two dishes: one for food and the other for water. A caique needs three: one for dry food, one for water, and a third for vegetables and fruits. Vegetables and fruits are an essential part of any caique's diet, but if they are left at room temperature too long, they become breeding grounds for potentially harmful bacteria, which could, in turn, contaminate the dry food if they were kept in the same dish.

In general, the dishes that come with the cage will work fine. Heavy plastic, stainless

CHECKLIST

Things to Do Before You Bring Your Bird Home

✔ Find an avian veterinarian and make an appointment to have your bird examined as soon as possible after you purchase it.

✔ Buy a suitable cage, assemble it if necessary, and place it in an appropriate spot in your home.

✔ Find out what the bird is accustomed to eating, and purchase a supply of that particular brand of food.

✔ Purchase at least three unbreakable dishes, if the cage did not come equipped with them.

✔ Purchase a cuttlebone or mineral block and install it in the cage near a perch so that the bird can have easy access to it.

✔ Purchase a large supply of toys and place most of them inside the cage, leaving a few out to be introduced later as the bird becomes bored with or destroys the first round of toys.

✔ If your bird is accustomed to drinking from a water bottle or you plan to use a water bottle, purchase one and install it so that the bird will be able to reach the tip easily.

✔ If your bird is not going to have access to direct sunlight, purchase a full-spectrum light to set up near the cage.

✔ Buy a suitable carrier for transporting your bird.

steel, and ceramic are all safe materials for your bird's dishes. Be sure to wash out the dishes with hot, soapy water before using them.

A type of dish that may pose a hazard is one that sits inside a ring that is fixed to the side of the cage. The dishes themselves do not pose a danger, but there are reports of birds trying to fit through the empty ring while the owner has the dish out to fill it. These birds may become stuck inside the ring and consequently damage their wings or legs trying to extricate themselves. Some birds have had to have their damaged wings amputated as a result of these injuries. If you do use a cage with this ring-and-dish type of arrangement, either remove the entire apparatus, ring, dish, and all every time you go to empty and refill the dish, or remove the dish from the ring, but take the bird with you while you go about cleaning and refilling it.

Be careful not to set up the cage so that the dishes are beneath a perch—you don't want the bird to defecate or drop debris into its food or water.

Lighting

Like people, birds absorb some of the vitamins they need from exposure to sunlight. This is particularly true of vitamin D_3, which is especially important for helping the birds absorb calcium, which in return results in stronger bones and better overall health. A major difficulty for most pet birds is that they do not get exposure to direct sunlight—they are kept indoors for their own safety, but the glass in most windows filters out the ultraviolet light they need.

If you live in a warmer climate, this situation can be easily resolved by allowing the bird to spend time in front of a window that has the glass section opened but the screen securely in place. If you live in an area where it's too cold much of the time to allow the window to remain open, you can meet your bird's lighting needs by purchasing a full spectrum light and setting it up so that it shines on your bird on a daily basis.

Full-spectrum lights are available at pet stores or through many pet supply catalogs and will emit the essential forms of light that your caique needs to maintain optimum health. The lights are available in either bulb or tube forms but are different from ordinary incandescent, fluorescent, and neon lights, which emit only a limited portion of the lighting spectrum. Full-spectrum lights are also different from heat lamps. The proper lighting will say "full spectrum" on the package.

These lights should be set up so that both the light and its cord are secured well out of your caique's reach. Follow package directions about how far away the light should be from the bird and exactly how many hours a day your bird should be exposed to its rays.

Cuttlebones and Mineral Blocks

Cuttlebones and mineral blocks both offer sources of calcium that your bird needs to maintain strong bones and, in the case of female caiques, to lay eggs. Cuttlebones are actually the bones of a small squidlike sea creature. They are an excellent source of calcium, but are much softer than commercially made mineral blocks, and an enthusiastic caique may reduce a cuttlebone to a pile of dust and rubble in a matter of minutes. Cuttlebones have a chalky side and a smoother,

shinier side. When you attach the cuttlebone to the side of the cage, place it so that the smoother side faces the bars and the softer, chalky side faces the bird and the interior of the cage.

Mineral blocks are more beak-resistant, but still offer an excellent source of calcium. They also have the advantage of being a bit easier to affix to the side of the cage than the irregularly shaped cuttlebone. Many brands of mineral block come artificially flavored like fruits and vegetables to encourage your bird to chew on them. Care should be taken not to place cuttlebones and mineral blocks directly underneath a perch or dish so that they won't become soiled by the bird's droppings.

Cuttlebones and mineral blocks are especially important for female caiques because they may lay eggs. Even a single caique hen who does not have access to a male may occasionally lay eggs, although, of course, such eggs will not be fertile and will never hatch. Because one never knows for sure whether a female caique is going to lay eggs, it is very important that it has access to one of these sources of calcium at all times, because its body will use the calcium in forming the shell.

Gravel and Grit

Some types of birds will swallow seeds whole, so they need to ingest sand or small pebbles to help them break down the husks inside their crops. This is true of birds such as turkeys and chickens, but it is not the case with caiques. Caiques are able to manipulate their food with their feet, beaks, and tongues, so are able to remove the husks and shells from the seeds that they eat before they swallow

Caiques enjoy both hanging toys and foot toys.

them. Caiques, therefore, do not require gravel and grit to digest their food.

Although many pet stores persist in carrying gravel and grit and marketing it as an essential need for the birds that they sell, no member of the parrot family—including parakeets, cockatiels, and bigger parrots—actually need gravel or grit. In fact, offering it to your bird may actually be dangerous. These products may become clogged inside the bird's digestive tract and in extreme cases may result in the bird's death. Therefore, you should never offer gravel or similar products to your caique.

Toys

Caiques *need* their toys.

A busy caique is a happy caique, and perhaps more than any other parrot, caiques love to

play. Toys help alleviate boredom, keep the caique's beak worn down, and provide mental stimulation. To keep a caique without toys is cruel. One has to watch a caique for only a very short time to see how much use and enjoyment it gets from playing with its toys.

Toys come in a variety of colors, shapes, and materials. Wooden toys are particularly beneficial because they help to keep the bird's beak worn down and to satisfy the bird's natural inclination to chew, making it slightly less likely that your caique will try chewing your wooden furniture. The precise type of toy that a caique prefers depends mostly on the individual caique. Some prefer hanging toys that they can swing on like miniature Tarzans, others, toys that they can manipulate with their feet, carry around, and toss about the cage. Your caique may develop a preference for a particular model, color, or toy made of a particular material. The only way to know for sure is by offering your caique a large selection of toys and seeing which ones it prefers.

Arrange hanging toys on the ceiling and sides of the cage. Try not to place the toys too close together in the cage. Caiques like to literally hang off their toys when they play with them, and you need to allow them enough space to do so. But you also need to make sure the bird has enough room to fly unimpeded from one side of the cage to the other, because even a clipped bird will be able to gain some forward motion in the air.

Foot toys are those that are not attached to the cage and can be picked up and manipulated by beak and foot. Caiques have a great

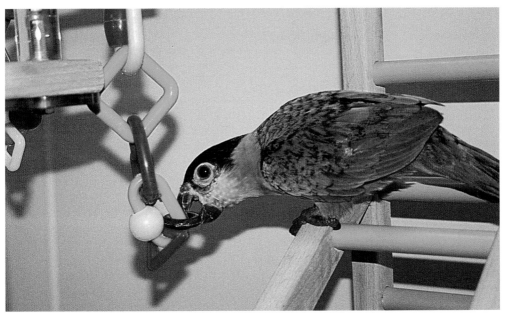

An ideal play stand will have a variety of easily accessible toys.

fondness for foot toys, and will pick them up, carry them around the cage, toss them, and even lie on their backs to juggle them with their feet. The drawback to foot toys is that they tend to get left on the floor of the cage where the caique may defecate on them. One solution might be to keep foot toys for use during the bird's out-of-cage time, placing them on the cage roof where the bird can play with them. But be warned: some caiques favorite game is to drop their toys off the top of their cage and see how many times they can get their owners to pick them up!

Some things to watch out for in toys are small parts that may come loose and be swallowed, "jingle" bells—small bells that have slits in them that can get caught on or cut probing tongues and toes, and toys hanging on *S* clips

with open ends that the birds can get caught on. You should inspect toys often to make sure that they are still safe. Tug on bell clappers and beads to make sure they are not coming loose, beware of sharp or splintered bits of wood, and remove any toy that looks like it's seen better days. Beware of clips that have open ends. The ideal is a toy strung on leather or cotton rope that can be tied to the cage roof, or one with a type of metal clip called a quick link that has a small screw-type closure that completely covers the opening so that the bird can't get caught on it.

Smart owners will have a large supply of bird toys but won't place all of them in the cage at the same time. They will rotate the selection, keeping some of the toys away from the bird and then using them to replace the ones in the

━━━━━━━━━━━ TIP ━━━━━━━━━━━

As far as caiques are concerned, you can never have too big a cage or too many toys.

cage once or twice a week. This will help make the toys last longer, because they won't be chewed and worn down as quickly as they would if the bird had nonstop access to them, and it will help keep the bird from becoming bored.

You can either buy bird toys ready made or make your own. Making toys for the family caique is a great way to involve children who might be too young to be allowed to handle the bird. Toys can be made from pieces salvaged from older toys, old car keys, wooden blocks (which can be colored and flavored by soaking them in a mixture of one package of sugar-free gelatin and two tablespoons of water—birds, like people, can perceive colors and are more attracted to colorful toys than to plain ones), heavy plastic beads, pieces of leather, shoelaces, cotton rope, and other beak-proof household items.

A Resting Place

Most caiques seem to enjoy having a place to snuggle into and sleep for the night. It may be that they feel more secure when they are able to get out of plain sight while they rest. There are several different types of resting places available in stores. Most are made of cloth, have a solid bottom for the bird to stand on, and come with attachments to hang them from the cage's ceiling. If you are handy with a needle and thread, you can try to sew one

yourself. I used an 18 × 12 inch (46 × 30 cm) rectangle of material, hemmed the edges, then sewed the shorter edges together to make a tube. I then cut an 11 × 6 inch (28 × 15 cm) piece of thick cardboard and inserted it into the tube so that when I pulled up the center of the tube, it formed a triangular "tent" with the cardboard as the floor. I then used a piece of thin cotton rope to hang the tent from the cage ceiling by running the rope through the tube and tying it into place by tying the ends of the rope to the bars at the top of the cage.

It may take your caique a while to realize that it can explore and enter this sleeping place. If so, be patient. You should also be sure to attach the sleeping space as close to the roof of the cage as you can manage, so that there's not enough room for the caique to perch on top of it, because if the caique decides to use its sleeping space as a perch, it will defecate down the sides, creating an unsightly, unsanitary mess.

Play Stands

Play stands are optional with caiques, although if you purchase a large, difficult-to-move cage, you might want to have a play stand set up in a different room so that you have a place to put your caique down if you want to keep it with you as you move around the house. There are a variety of commercial play stands available, with an assortment of perches, ladders, and swings for the bird's entertainment. It may take several attempts before you can convince the bird that it needs to stay on the play stand rather than getting down to go exploring, but if you consistently return the bird to its cage every time it gets down onto the floor, it should eventually

Caique toys can be store-bought or homemade.

understand that if it wants to stay in your presence, it needs to remain on the stand.

As an alternative to commercially available play stands, I use a collapsible wooden clothes drying rack. I set the rack up over newspapers and tie an assortment of toys to the various rungs. Dishes for food and water can also be attached. This arrangement is much less expensive than the commercial models and has the advantage of being easily collapsible, so I can just remove the dishes and fold the entire thing up to store in the closet if I'm having guests over. The one disadvantage is that the wooden rungs are subject to chewing by the caique. I need to replace my makeshift stand a couple of times a year, but I find that the convenience of storage and portability make it worthwhile for both me and my birds.

YOUR CAIQUE'S DIET

It used to be thought that all you needed to feed a bird was bird seed. This was sufficient to keep the bird alive for a few years, but it was a far cry from a nutritious diet. As scientists have learned more about avian nutrition, caiques' diets have gotten better and better. As a result, captive caiques are now living longer than ever before.

A Balanced Diet

A nutritious diet may be the single best thing you can do to improve your bird's health and quality of life. If you have a bird that comes to you already eating a healthful, well-balanced diet, thank your lucky stars. If you have a bird whose diet is lacking, you may have an uphill battle trying to persuade it to eat better, but if you can manage it, you may be adding years to your bird's life.

Because the first days in your home are a time of major transition and upheaval, it's best to allow your caique to remain on the diet it's accustomed to, at least in the beginning. If you buy your bird at a pet store, purchase a supply of the food it's accustomed to. If your bird comes from a breeder or as a secondhand pet, ask what brand of food it usually eats and try to have it on hand when you bring the bird home.

A healthy diet is a key step in having a healthy caique.

An ideal parrot diet consists of pellets, fresh fruits and vegetables, and a small amount of nuts or seeds. Caiques should also always have access to a supply of clean water.

Pellets

Pellets are a relatively new invention. They are a manufactured food designed to be as nutritionally complete as possible. They come in a variety of colors, flavors, shapes, and sizes. A caique would do best with medium pellets, which are also sometimes labeled as being "for conure sized birds."

Although pellets are markedly more expensive than seed mix, they are less fattening, more nutritionally complete, and create less waste and mess than traditional seed mix because the entire pellet can be eaten—you don't end up paying for the shells and husks that will be dropped after the bird has opened them. They may also result in a bird with fewer health problems, which can save you a large

Like most of us, caiques really enjoy their food.

amount of money and heartache in the long run.

The disadvantage to pellets is that many birds seem to prefer the taste of seeds and may refuse to eat them. Most packages of pellets come with a variety of suggestions about how you can "convert" your bird to a pelleted diet. It's not a good idea to try to force your bird to eat pellets by withholding all other forms of food. If a caique has never seen a pellet before, it may not recognize it as food and may actually go hungry in spite of the fact that it has this new type of food in its dish. I sometimes sneak the pellets into a reluctant bird's diet by baking them into

a batch of "birdie bread" so that the bird begins to get used to the taste of them during the transition. (See the sidebar, page 35, for a recipe.)

You may need to experiment with different brands and flavors of pellets until you find one that your caique prefers. It may take time and patience, but be persistent. Your bird's health depends on it.

Fruits and Vegetables

Fruits and vegetables are an important part not only of your own diet, but of a healthy bird's diet as well. Although fresh fruits and vegetables are best, frozen and thawed vegetables or canned vegetables are acceptable as well. (Note: Always opt for salt-free packaged vegetables.) Caiques generally seem to prefer vegetables to fruits, although each individual bird will have its own preferences. Leftover vegetables from your dinner are perfectly acceptable, provided that you did not salt them. The greater the variety of fruits and vegetables you can provide, the more balanced the bird's diet will be.

One thing that the owner should be aware of, however, is that vegetables and fruits—indeed, any moist food—should not be left in the bird's dish for more than an hour or two. Their moist surfaces at room temperature become perfect breeding grounds for potentially harmful bacteria. Be sure to remove any uneaten fruits or vegetables from your bird's dish within a couple of hours.

A particular effort should be made to include foods that are high in vitamin A in your caique's diet. Many caiques suffer from a lack of this vitamin, which is found in high concentrations in dark green leafy and yellow vegetables.

Whether or not you want to cut your bird's fresh food into caique-sized portions before serving it is up to you. Some people think that this makes it easier for the bird; others reason that no one cuts up the bird's food in the wild, so it can manage whole foods just fine. A fussy eater, or one that seems reluctant to try new foods, may be more likely to try them if they are presented differently—cut into chunks instead of thin slices, for example, or placed between the bars of the cage rather than served in a dish. Persistence is often the key, and a bird who refuses to eat a particular food for months may suddenly begin to eat as if that were its favorite food in the world. You can also

The greater the variety of fruits and vegetables your caique eats, the healthier it will be.

encourage your bird to try a new food by eating it in front of the bird and making a big fuss about how good it is, then offering a bite. If it's a food that the bird has never seen before, it may need this practical demonstration before it realizes that the green-colored thing is actually meant to be eaten. Just be sure never to offer your caique food that has actually been in contact with your mouth—human mouths contain bacteria that is harmful to birds.

One major exception to the general rule that all fruits and vegetables are safe to give your bird is the avocado. Avocados and anything containing avocados should never be offered

Wet and dry foods should be kept in separate dishes.

to your caique. Although safe for humans, avocados contain a substance that is poisonous to members of the parrot family. If you keep avocados in your house, make sure that every member of your family is aware that they can be deadly to the bird, and they are kept well away from the bird in all circumstances.

Heat-and-Eat Mixes

"Heat-and-eat" food mixes are packages of dried foods that are sold in pet stores. They generally contain dried pasta, rice, or beans, and an assortment of dried fruits, vegetables, nuts, and seeds. Water is added and they are slowly cooked until they are rehydrated and tender; then they are served to the bird.

Although they are not a necessity, these mixes do make a tasty treat for your bird. Most packages contain instructions for cooking either a small amount at a time or the whole package all at once. For convenience sake, you might want to cook the entire package, then portion the excess into an ice-cube tray for

freezing. Store the frozen food cubes in a plastic bag in the freezer, and heat one or two of them in the microwave for your caique's daily treat. I particularly like to do this for my birds on winter mornings, serving them a warm breakfast (be careful not to put piping-hot food into your caique's dish). Because they do not contain anything harmful for your bird, these treats can be offered daily, but any leftovers should be removed from the cage after an hour or two to avoid spoiling.

Table Foods

Few things interest caiques as much as watching you eat. They will whistle, chirp, and bounce up and down to capture your attention and, they hope, score a bite of whatever it is that you're eating. Some people are hesitant to feed their caique "people food," but as a general rule, what's good for you is good for your bird.

Foods such as pasta, rice, unsalted fruits and vegetables, whole-grain breads, cooked eggs, and snacks such as unsalted popcorn and crackers are fine to feed your caique. Avoid dairy products, especially milk, because it contains lactose, which birds are not able to digest. Thoroughly cooked meats, such as chicken and fish, can be given occasionally in very small amounts. Wild caiques eat insects, so it's thought that the protein found in meat may be beneficial.

Foods that should be avoided are those that contain salt, caffeine, or alcohol or are high in fats. You should not offer to share your potato chips, coffee, tea, chocolate, or beer with your caique. As mentioned before, avocado and avocado products should also be strictly avoided.

Seeds and Nuts

The traditional ingredients of bird food mixes are actually not that nutritious. Seeds are high in fat and limited in the number and amounts of vitamins and minerals that they offer. Eating nothing but seeds is the avian equivalent of a junk-food diet. Although many veterinarians recommend not feeding caiques any seed at all, it can be given as a special treat, or a small amount can be given daily in addition to pellets.

Nuts in the shell are a special favorite of caiques both as playthings and as snacks.

Some caiques are especially fond of dropping food and toys into their drinking water.

Almonds are a particular favorite, and offering your new bird an almond every time you approach the cage during the first few days it lives with you can be a great way to create a favorable impression.

Giving the bird the nuts in the shell rather than already shelled helps to stimulate the bird mentally, alleviates boredom, and helps keep the beak worn down, just as they do for wild caiques.

Water

Water is as essential to a caique as it is to a human being. Fresh, clean water should be available to your bird at all times. In general, ordinary tap water is fine for a caique. However, if for some reason you would hesitate to

Caiques are notoriously messy eaters—what doesn't end up inside the caique is likely to end up either on the bird or on the floor.

drink the tap water yourself, you might want to use bottled water for your bird instead.

One caution about your caique's water: some caiques seem to think that it's fun to drop things into their water dish, which results in dirty water. If your bird falls into this category, check the water frequently to make sure that it's clean. If you find toys or food floating in the water dish, remove them and replace the water. Some people try to head off this problem by providing their bird with a water bottle instead of a dish. This is an effective solution, but the bird should be watched carefully for the first few days to ensure that it figures out how to drink from the bottle. If the bird doesn't seem to be using it, go back to the water dish that the bird is accustomed to.

As is the case with the food dishes, the positioning of the water dish is important. It should not be beneath a perch, to avoid having the bird's droppings fall into the water.

Feeding

When and how much you feed your caique is not as important as the fact that it must have access to food and clean water 24 hours a day, seven days a week. If you have fairly large dishes and fill them once a day, this may be sufficient, or you may need to refill the dish when you get home from work or later in the evening. My own birds get a dish full of dry food (a mix of pellets and a lesser amount of seeds) in the morning, and then a serving of fruits and vegetables shortly after I get home from work. This allows me to be home to remove these moist foods before they can spoil.

If you are feeding your bird a diet of mostly seed mix while trying to change over to a pellet diet, do not assume that because the dish looks like it still has something in it, it still contains food. Because caiques remove the shells and husks from seeds, many of these indigestible pieces will be dropped back into the dish. Don't mistake these leavings for food—the bird cannot eat them.

What NOT to Feed Your Caique

In addition to avocados, which were discussed previously, there are several foods that are either unhealthful or toxic for your bird. These include foods that contain alcohol, caffeine (including coffee, many teas, and chocolate), and foods that are high in fat or salt. Milk is also a no-no, although dairy products that do not contain lactose, such as yogurt, are not harmful. As a general rule, if a food is considered "junk food" for you, it's also junk food for your bird and should not be fed to it. The

Birdie Bread Recipe

This recipe is a big favorite at my house. Adding a baby food jar of carrots or sweet potatoes instead of water not only makes it tastier, but provides your bird with a healthful extra dose of vitamin A. Adding the crushed eggshell creates a source of calcium. Because of the eggshells, the bread is not recommended for human consumption.

1 8½-ounce box of corn muffin mix
1 6-ounce jar of baby food (carrot or sweet potatoes work well in this recipe)
1 egg, including the shell
1 cup of frozen mixed vegetables
½ cup of pelleted bird food

Grease 6 muffin pans or a small (approximately 4 × 6 inch) loaf pan. In a medium-size bowl, combine the corn muffin mix and baby food. Mix well. Add the egg, then crush the shell into small pieces and add it to the mixture as well (you can either crush it in your bare hand or place it in a baggie and break it up that way). Add the pellets and vegetables (it's not necessary to cook or defrost them first). Bake in a 350°F oven for 20 minutes for muffins or 30 minutes for a loaf. Cool before serving.

Extra birdie bread can be frozen for later use.

more healthful you can make the bird's diet, the healthier your bird will be.

Vitamin Supplements

You may notice a variety of different vitamin supplements available in the bird supply aisle of your pet store and be tempted to use them to improve your caique's overall health. Don't bother. If your bird eats a healthful diet that includes pellets and an assortment of vegetables, then it is probably getting all the vitamins it needs. Vitamins that are meant to be dissolved in the bird's water supply will promote the growth of harmful bacteria, spoiling the water. Vitamins that are intended to be sprinkled on the bird's food supply are likely to just trickle down between the pieces, gathering at the bottom of the dish where they are not eaten.

If, for some reason, your avian veterinarian does recommend a vitamin or mineral supplement, the best way to get it into your bird is to feed the bird a moist, cooked food, such as a heat-and-eat mix or mashed vegetables. The vitamins will stick to the food and be eaten along with it.

Caiques may eat more than you would expect for such a small bird—they eat to keep their energy level high.

Choosing a caique is not an easy undertaking. Whatever bird you choose may be a part of your household for many years to come. It's important to take your time to find the bird whose personality will fit well with yours. If you're extremely lucky, you'll happen upon a bird who makes it very clear that it wants you. If not, there are steps that you can take to help you in your search for the perfect caique for you.

Finding the Perfect Bird

You've read everything you can get your hands on and decided that caiques are the perfect pet for you. You've bought a cage, hung the toys, found an avian veterinarian, and are finally ready. Now all you need is the bird.

Although caiques are still somewhat uncommon and can be difficult to find, there are several possible ways to acquire one. Buying a bird directly from a breeder or a pet store, or acquiring a secondhand bird from a shelter or a private party each offer potential pros and cons, but an informed consumer can navigate these options to find his or her ideal bird. The more you know, the better off you will be.

The best choice as a pet is the caique who seems to pick you.

Black Heads, White Bellies

Other than appearance and a slight difference in size, the two different species of caique are remarkably similar in terms of personality and pet potential. Because neither species makes a better pet than the other, it may come down to a question of which one you find more attractive or simply what is available when you go to look. White-bellied caiques tend to be a bit more expensive than their black-headed cousins, simply because breeders are less successful in coaxing white-bellied caiques to reproduce.

Males and Females

Caiques are sexually monomorphic, which means that you can't tell a male from a female simply by looking at it. A simple test is available, which uses a sample of blood or freshly plucked

Questions to Ask Before Buying Your Caique

1. How old is the bird, and is it weaned?
2. Does the bird know how to "step up" onto a hand if requested to do so?
3. Does the bird come with any kind of health guarantee?
4. What kind of diet is the caique on? What brand of food does it eat?
5. Has the bird's sex been determined?
6. Has the bird been vaccinated against polyoma virus?
7. If it's an older bird, what is its history and why is it available for sale now?
8. If I have any questions or problems after I bring the bird home, can I call on you for help?

chest feathers to examine the bird's DNA and determine its sex. This can be done either by a veterinarian or by using a special kit that you can send for from a laboratory that does such testing. A veterinarian can use a laparoscope to examine the bird's internal organs to determine whether it possesses ovaries or testicles, but this procedure involves anesthetizing the bird and making an incision in the skin to insert the laparoscope and is not without some risk to the bird. The third, and most time-honored method of discovering a caique's sex is to wait and see if the bird lays an egg—a sure sign of a female, although, of course, not all hens will lay eggs and even if they do, there is no chance that the egg will hatch unless the hen has had access to a male caique.

In terms of pet potential, the difference between males and females seems to be very slight. Females may be at risk of becoming egg bound, but this is not a frequent occurrence. Either sex has the potential to make a cherished and suitable pet.

Some breeders and pet stores have their birds sexed as a matter of course, others do not. If you prefer one sex over another, you may have to do a bit of extra searching to find it. Some places will ask you to pay for DNA testing, but will not refund the cost if the chick tested does not turn out to be the sex you wanted.

Breeders

One of the best ways to acquire a caique is to buy it directly from a breeder. If you don't know of a caique breeder in your area, you can find one online or by reading the classified ads in the back of a national bird magazine. Breeders have the advantage of knowing their birds. A really good breeder might ask you about your preferences and lifestyle and steer you toward a particular bird whose personality seems to be more compatible with your needs.

A good breeder will be selling healthy, hand-fed baby caiques who are fully weaned at the time of sale. Avoid anyone who tries to sell you an unweaned bird, telling you that the baby will bond better with you if you're the one to hand-feed it. Hand-feeding a baby bird is a complicated, risky undertaking and not something for an amateur to attempt. A reputable breeder will not let you have the baby bird until it is eating completely on its own and maintaining its body weight.

Breeders also have the advantage of generally lower prices than a pet store. A breeder should be willing to provide references from other people who have purchased baby birds from him or her. You should also ask if the breeder offers a guarantee on the birds and exactly what that guarantee entails. Reputable breeders will stand behind their birds and will probably offer a limited guarantee on their health.

If you are unable to find a caique breeder in your area, you may be able to find one who is willing to ship his or her birds across the country by plane. In many cases, this works out very well, but proceed with caution. If the bird arrives and proves to have an existing health problem, you may have to ship to the breeder to enforce the guarantee, and the shipping is at your own expense. Conceivably you could end up having to pay shipping both ways and still have no bird to show for it.

Pet Stores

Pet stores are pretty much a hit-or-miss proposition. Some are excellent, reputable, and staffed with truly knowledgeable people, whereas others are less reputable, unsanitary, and may sell animals who come with significant health or behavioral problems. They also generally charge more than breeders because they have to pay the additional expenses that come with owning, stocking, and staffing a store.

It's not hard to tell a good pet store from a poor one. You can tell a lot by looking. Are the cages roomy and clean, the dishes full, and the animals lively and interactive? When you talk to the staff, do they know a lot about the animals they sell and their care? Do they offer a guarantee on their merchandise and have a regular veterinarian who they use in case one of the animals develops a health problem? A poor store will be marked by overcrowded cages, dull, listless-looking animals, piles of excrement, and an indifferent staff. As tempt-

A well-socialized caique should know the command to "step up" before you buy it.

ing as it is to want to "rescue" a bird from a situation like this, it's just not a good idea. The store owner will merely replace the bird with another one, and you will be stuck with a bird who probably has significant health and behavioral issues. The better thing to do is to contact your local animal control office and report what you have seen. Animal control may have the authority to seize the animals and to fine the store owners.

As is the case with breeders, a good pet store will not let you take home an unweaned baby bird. They will also offer you some sort of health guarantee. Watch the staff when they interact with the bird. Do they talk to the bird and make eye contact with it? Does the bird seem comfortable when handled? Does the staff know the answers to whatever questions you might have about caiques in general and the bird you're interested in in particular?

A pet store offers the advantage of allowing you to visit the bird at your convenience, giving you a chance to get to know it before you decide to purchase it.

As this breeding pair of black-headed caiques demonstrates, you can't tell the males from the females based on their appearance.

Secondhand Birds

Acquiring a secondhand bird is a bit of a gamble. You may find yourself taking in a bird who is already well socialized and friendly, or you may find yourself taking in a bird whose behavior was too difficult for the previous owner to endure.

Before taking in a secondhand bird, ask why the bird is being given up. It could be for a perfectly legitimate reason—for example the bird was found but efforts to trace the owner were unsuccessful and the finder cannot keep it, or the previous owner died or became unable to care for the bird any longer. In my house we have two birds who came to us as adults. One was abandoned at the veterinarian's and spent the next five years there in a cat cage before we were asked to take her, and another came to us when her owner of 11 years had to go into a nursing home. Both of them are as sweet and gentle as you could hope for a pet to be.

On the other hand, if the previous owner no longer wants the bird because of a behavior problem, such as excessive noise or biting, you will want to proceed with caution. This isn't to say that a bird who is given up for behavioral reasons will never make a suitable pet. What's excessive noise to one person may merely be background noise to another, or there may be something about the environment that makes the bird react in an undesirable fashion.

The best thing to do when considering a secondhand bird is to meet it. Does the reason stated for wanting to give up the bird seem to be a valid one? Can you live with the bird and its circumstances? Are you willing to work with the bird to help modify its behavior?

Birds that are lost and found pose a special problem. Not only is there no history on the bird, but it's possible that it picked up some sort of illness during its time in the wild. A found bird should be checked by an avian veterinarian to ensure that it is healthy, particularly if you already have pet birds in the house.

Guarantees

Most reputable sellers will stand behind the health of their birds. Always ask if there is a

Two caiques will keep each other amused while their owners work during the day.

guarantee and exactly what the requirements of that guarantee are before you buy any bird. How long do you have to get the bird checked by an avian veterinarian? Will the seller reimburse you for any medical expenses that the bird incurs, or will you have to surrender the bird for a replacement or refund? If the bird was shipped to you and found to be ill, who will pay to have the bird shipped back to the seller if that's one of the conditions of the guarantee?

Always try to get the guarantee in writing—it may be difficult to enforce otherwise.

Shipping

Because caiques are still fairly uncommon, you may have a difficult time trying to find one available in your area. If this is the case, you may have to resort to a breeder from another part of the country. Although it's always risky to buy anything sight unseen, the actual shipping is surprisingly safe. Be sure to check the seller's references carefully and listen closely to how they answer your questions. If you feel comfortable enough to buy a bird from them, you may be asked to put a deposit on the bird if it's still unweaned and pay off the balance when it's ready to go. The bird will be shipped once the final payment has cleared. Never wire money to a stranger or to a stranger's bank account—that makes it too hard to get proof of payment if the seller is disreputable. Generally, a deposit can be paid by personal check, and the balance paid by bank check or money order so that the seller can be assured that the check won't bounce and will be able to ship your bird as soon as possible.

Birds have to have a health certificate signed by a veterinarian before an airline will accept them for shipping. Don't take this health certificate as proof that you're acquiring a thriving, disease-free bird. An airline health certificate does not require the same battery of tests and as thorough an exam as your veterinarian will give the bird during its first visit, and birds are extremely good at hiding illnesses. Basically, a health certificate ensures only that the bird was alive when the veterinarian saw it.

The breeder will make reservations for the bird's airplane flight in advance and will let you

know the date and flight number. Because the bird will fly in the cargo section of the plane and not all planes have pressurized cargo bays, the airlines will have restrictions on which flights a bird can be shipped on. In some cases, an airport may not have any incoming flights to a particular area where the planes have pressurized cargo areas. If this is the case, the bird will not be able to be flown to the airport closest to you and you may have to meet your bird for the first time at a different airport.

Airlines have certain requirements for the containers a bird must be shipped in. They have to meet certain size regulations and be made of a strong enough material to withstand other packages falling on top of them in transit. With a bird, they also require some sort of perch in the container, although with a young caique, the bird is more likely to stand on the floor and hold on to the perch with its beak rather than to sit on it. Because dishes can spill in transit, the safest way to provide nourishment during the flight is to have a variety of foods on the carrier floor for the bird to snack on. This is generally not a very sanitary practice, but in most cases the bird will be in the carrier only a few hours. The shipper should try to include enough fruits, vegetables, and nuts for several days, however, in case something goes wrong during shipping and the bird is not able to get to its destination in a timely manner. Fruits, such as grapes and berries, that do not have a moist exposed edge are the most resistant to harboring bacteria and contain juices that can keep your bird hydrated in the absence of a water dish. These foods will tide the bird over if it misses a connecting flight or if, for some reason, the flight is diverted and grounded unexpectedly.

Brighter plumage and lighter colored eyes distinguish adults from juveniles.

No matter where you purchase your caique, you should look for birds that are alert and comfortable being approached and handled by people.

Airline regulations will not allow the bird to be shipped if extreme temperatures are forecast anywhere along the route. For the purposes of shipping birds, "cold weather" is defined as below 50°F (10°C). If temperatures are variable during the time of year that your bird is being shipped, be aware that plans may have to change if the weather en route suddenly turns colder or hotter on the day you intend to have the bird flown to you.

When the breeder takes the bird to the airport to be shipped, he or she will be given a shipping number that can be used to track the bird's progress. The breeder will call you once he or she has this number, because you will

need to know it to retrieve your caique. This helps to protect your bird from theft, because strangers who see the bird on the counter will not be able to claim that the bird is theirs unless they know that shipping number.

The best way to ship the bird is counter to counter. This generally means that your bird will be carried out to you as soon as the plane lands rather than you having to wait until all the baggage is unloaded first.

When the breeder calls to tell you the shipping number, ask if there is anything special that you will need to open the carrier. Some breeders put a combination lock on the cage and tell you the combination over the phone to discourage theft, and some shipping containers may be screwed shut so that you can't open them without a screwdriver. It's best not to open the container until you have the bird safely at home, and birds should never be allowed loose in the car when you are driving, even if you have another person along to hold it.

Actual shipping experiences can vary widely. Most of the time I've had birds shipped to me, the process has gone off without a hitch. On one occasion, however, the bird missed a connecting flight and was ten hours late, and she apparently spent ten hours in a baggage area in New Jersey next to a barking Doberman Pinscher that had missed the same connection. When the bird finally did arrive, it was very late at night and she was a nervous wreck from listening to her traveling companion bark for hours on end. It took her a long time to calm down, and she eventually became a trusting and loving pet. In most cases, however, shipping a bird is safe and goes smoothly.

Picking Out Your Caique

It may be that you've carefully researched many different types of parrots and come to the conclusion that a caique is your ideal bird, or it may be that you happened across a caique in a pet store and were attracted to its playful, active demeanor. If you are very lucky, you'll meet a bird that wants you. It will follow you every time you walk past the cage, may call you when you walk away from it, and leans desperately toward you whenever someone else is holding it, making it clear that it would rather be with you. If this happens to you, count yourself lucky. Some of the best owner-pet relationships start this way. If this happens to you and

you decide that you want the bird and are in a position to provide it with a good and nurturing home, then the bird's species, sex, or age won't matter—you'll have found your ideal bird. Other people may have to work a little harder to find the caique of their dreams.

Whether you stumble across the bird you want or you have to search to find it, you want to make sure to begin with a healthy bird. Buying a bird sight unseen and having it shipped puts the buyer at a major disadvantage. Although you can't tell if a bird is healthy just by observing it, there are some signs of illness that you can spot and that will let you know that the bird is definitely *not* healthy.

A healthy caique is an active caique. Look for a bird that is awake and seems to be alert and curious about the world around it. A bird who sits half crouched on the perch or cage floor, whose feathers are puffed out rather than smooth against its body, or whose eyes have a glazed or half-closed look is to be avoided. A healthy caique will be playing with its toy or cage mates, or moseying over to the side of the cage to check you out. The vent area should be clean and dry, and the droppings that you see on the bottom of the cage should be solid, not watery, and well-formed coils of dark green laced with white (although some foods, such as beets, will alter the color of the bird's droppings).

Because birds tend to hide all signs of illness for as long as they are physically able, you should also look at the bird's surroundings for clues to its health. Poor hygiene is a sign that the bird may not be completely healthy. If you are not completely satisfied with the look of the bird or its surroundings, then by all means do not purchase that particular bird.

Choosing which individual bird to buy can be a daunting task.

Beginning with a healthy bird will save you a lot of grief and hundreds of dollars in veterinary costs. Ask the seller if your caique has been vaccinated against Polyoma virus, particularly if he or she operates a fairly large aviary. Caiques tend to be more susceptible to this disease than other birds, and it's one of the few avian diseases for which there is an inoculation. A smaller operation or a closed aviary whose birds are not exposed to other birds may not bother with this vaccine, but if your breeder has had his or her birds inoculated, it's another sign that you are buying from a reputable establishment.

Caiques are somewhat seasonal breeders, going to nest in the spring. For this reason, it may be easier to find a young caique available in the summer months than in the winter. Although slightly older caiques can make wonderful pets, it's great fun to watch a baby as it explores the world with wide-eyed enthusiasm.

Once you've found a seller whom you believe is reputable, it's time to meet the birds. Because the biggest difference between white-bellied and black-headed caiques is appearance, and because the behavioral differences between sexes are slight, your choice will probably come down to either personal preference in terms of appearance, or availability. Because black-headed breed slightly more easily in captivity than white-bellied, they are somewhat easier to find and a bit less expensive than their "blond" counterparts. Look at the photographs in this book. If the look of one species appeals to you more than the other, then by all means, make the effort to find that type of bird. If you are more flexible and appearance isn't as important as personality, then your decision may be dictated by what's available when you go looking.

When faced with a clutch of healthy, energetic caiques, it may be difficult to distinguish one from another. Ask the seller what each bird is like. If the birds were hand-fed, the seller should be able to tell you which baby is the quietest, or the snuggliest, or the most interactive. Don't be surprised if the seller asks you about your household and circumstances and tries to encourage you to consider a particular bird—he or she wants to make the best match possible.

If you are in a position where you have your heart set on a caique but you can't find a breeder in your area, you may have to use a breeder who is too far away for you to visit. If this is the case, there are still some things you can do to help ensure that you buy a healthy bird. Ask the seller for references, and the names of customers who have bought his or her birds and can attest to the reliability of the transaction and the health of the bird. Ask the seller if he or she will stand behind the birds and provide a copy of any guarantee in writing before you actually buy the caique.

In the end, the individual caique you choose may be a fairly arbitrary decision. You may decide on the one that insists on playing with your buttons, or the one that hustles to be the first one out of the cage when the door is open, or the one that hatched on your birthday. As long as you choose a healthy, well-socialized caique, you'll be off to a good start.

Bringing Home the Bird

Transitioning from one home to another can be fairly traumatic for some birds. Caiques seem to weather the change better than many other species, but it's still best to proceed slowly so that the bird doesn't feel overwhelmed by a bunch of strange people all wanting to interact with it the instant it gets out of its carrier. The best thing to do is to place your new caique directly in its new cage, so that it's not the center of all activity, but is close enough to observe the goings-on in its new home without feeling threatened. Some people make a point of having the seller place the bird in the carrier for the trip to its new home so that the bird won't associate you with the loss of its familiar environment. This may or may not be necessary, but it's something else to keep in mind if you're trying to make all possible efforts to be in your caique's good graces.

Try not to disturb the bird too much during its first hours in a new home. If the bird seems to be distressed when you go to interact with it, try to avoid making prolonged eye contact with it. When a wild caique is being stalked, the predator will stare unrelentingly at the bird as it makes its approach; consequently being stared at may make the bird uncomfortable. When you go to interact with the bird for the first few encounters, blink slowly and deliberately several times as a way of assuring the caique that you don't intend to harm it. If the bird is feeling comfortable with your presence, it may well blink back at you as a way of assuring you that it perceives no immediate threat. If the bird seems to get agitated when you approach, make a point of looking away for a few seconds to see if that helps to calm it.

Quarantine

Quarantine is necessary only if you already have birds in your house, or if you purchase two birds from different sources at the same time. Keeping the bird isolated from the other avian members of your household until you are certain that it doesn't carry any contagious diseases is one of the simplest and smartest things you can do to protect both your birds and your pocketbook. One sick bird can incur significant medical bills, two or more sick birds, especially when one of them is already your beloved, bonded pet, can be devastating. Quarantine should be observed whether or not your first bird is a caique—many avian diseases can be spread from one species to another.

If you are bringing your new caique into a home where there is already a bird in residence, try to choose a quarantine location as far away from the resident bird as possible. Opposite ends or floors of the house are good choices. If possible, choose rooms that do not share the same ventilation lines, particularly in the cooler months.

If you have a bird in quarantine, remember that several diseases can be transported by the caretaking human. Viruses can be transported when dust from dried droppings becomes airborne and settles upon the clothing and hands of the person who services the cages. For this reason, make a point to always attend to your old bird first, so that you do not unwittingly carry a virus from the new bird to the old one. Practice good hygiene. Always wash your hands thoroughly after you are finished attending to either bird.

Even a healthy looking bird can be harboring an illness, so observing quarantine and visiting the veterinarian are very important precautions.

If you have any reason to suspect that one of the birds has a health problem, contact your avian veterinarian immediately. You may also want to extend your hygienic practices so that you change your shoes and clothing after you attend to the suspect pet—viruses can be carried on them as well.

Quarantine should be observed for at least 30 days even if you get a clean bill of health from your avian veterinarian right after the bird is purchased, in case your new caique was exposed to something just before purchase and the illness hasn't had time to manifest itself. Quarantine should also be strictly observed if, at some point in the future, you decide to acquire a second bird.

MAINTAINING YOUR CAIQUE

With good nutrition, proper veterinary care, and a healthy dose of vigilance, your caique may be with you for as long as four decades. Caiques need a considerable amount of behavioral guidance to keep them the friendly, interactive pet that you want. This chapter will help you maintain a high-quality owner-pet relationship as well as familiarize you with some of the general maintenance tasks that you may need to perform to keep your caique happy and comfortable.

Behavior

Caiques are not easy birds in terms of behavior. They will frequently test their owner's status as "head of the flock" and may experience periods when their fluctuating hormones affect their moods. The keys to a well-behaved caique are clarity and consistency.

If a caique exhibits an undesirable behavior such as biting, excessive noise, or an obsession with a particular object, it should promptly be told "No," and an attempt should be made to

A healthy caique will be both active and attractive.

distract the bird by moving it to another setting or offering it a toy or some other object to hold its attention. If the caique persists in the undesired behavior, it should be returned to its cage and the owner should withdraw from the room. If this "time-out" is used consistently every time the bird misbehaves, most birds eventually figure out that if they want their owner's quality attention, then they need to refrain from undesirable behaviors.

I usually tell my birds why they are going back to their cages. I pick up the offending party, say, "Noisy birds go to bird jail," and then follow through with the consequence. Almost

Like small children, caiques will frequently test the boundaries of acceptable behavior.

establishing a degree of control. Many caiques will come to their new homes already knowing how to do this, but in case yours doesn't, gently nudge its belly with an upward motion, touching it just above the legs with the side of your index finger while telling it "Up" (the actual words you use can vary; I just use *up* because I find it short and to the point). The proper way to hold a caique is to allow it to stand on the side of your hand, with both your palm and the bird facing toward you. A well-socialized caique will come to you already knowing how to do this, but if you have a bird that is unfamiliar with the command, it should step up onto your hand if only to get you to stop nudging it. Eventually the word alone will suffice to get the bird to step onto a proffered hand.

A bird whose behavior is beginning to escalate and needs to be reined in can often be diverted by being given the command to "step up" from one hand to another repeatedly, as a reminder that its owner has a higher status in the "flock" and that it needs to behave accordingly. There are times when this strategy is effective and times when it's not appropriate. A bird that is truly angry or upset is just as likely to bite the hand as it is to step up on it. If this is the case, time-out is much better than the step-up strategy.

Birds who persist in an undesirable behavior should be checked by an avian veterinarian to make sure the behavior doesn't have a physical cause. If a bird has a cracked or broken bone, for example, it may well scream or try to bite you when you try to handle it. If this is the

all of my birds, under normal circumstances, now stop making the noise when they hear "Noisy birds go to bird jail," because they would rather stay out of their cage and interact with me than lose their out-of-cage time.

After five or ten minutes or so of time-out, the bird is given a second chance at proving that it can behave according to expectations. This has been so effective at my house that I once had an older bird lean down from my shoulder to peer at a fussy chick in my hand and say, quite clearly, "Go to bird jail!"

Teaching your caique to step up onto your hand early on is an excellent first step in

case, no amount of behavior modification will help until the bird's physical needs are taken care of.

It goes without saying that a misbehaving bird should never be punished physically. Hitting, yelling, shaking the cage, or throwing anything at the bird will only damage the owner-pet relationship and encourage the bird to bite and yell out of fear and anger. Such actions are abusive and should never be used.

If an undesirable behavior persists, the owner should try to look for a cause. Sometimes factors that the owner barely notices may be extremely upsetting for the caique and may quite possibly be what sets off the bird's behavior. Look for patterns in the bird's misbehavior. Does it occur only at a particular time of day? Does it happen only in a certain part of the house or with a certain pattern? Is there an unusual sound or activity going on when it happens?

Biting is not always the result of hostility or anger. It can also be the result of fear. Some caiques will actually bite their loved ones if they perceive a danger and want the loved one to flee—and in many cases, the loved one is the human owner. If you realize that your caique bites you every time there's a truck outside collecting the trash, it may well be the sound of the trash being compacted that's upsetting the bird. If your caique bites you when you go to put it into its cage before you go on a date, it may be that the blood-red nail polish that you wear only when you go out is what's alarming the bird. (Caiques, like all parrots, can perceive colors.) If your caique is sitting by the window and begins to fuss and throws itself off its perch, biting at you when you try to pick it up, it may be that it spotted a bird of

Caiques occasionally try to bathe in their water dishes.

prey outdoors and fears for its life. If your child recently brought a helium-filled balloon into the house, the sight of it may remind the caique of a bird of prey, and cause it to react in a blind panic.

There are also times when it's easier to remove the object that upsets or obsesses your caique rather than trying to alter the bird's behavior. Caiques can be very stubborn. In the cases above you can try moving the cage away from the street where the garbage truck stops, remove the nail polish, or pull the blinds.

It's not always possible for the owner to identify the cause of a bird's misbehavior—caiques see the world differently than humans do. In extreme cases, you can consult an "avian behavioralist." These people hire themselves out to analyze your home, bird, and situation and make suggestions about how to modify undesirable behaviors. If your bird's behavior is having such a negative effect on your home that you are seriously thinking of giving it up, you may want to look for an avian behavioral consultant first.

Because avian behavioralists are still fairly uncommon, you may need to do some research on the Internet to find one. Although most behavioralists prefer to visit a bird's home in person, many are also willing to do consultations over the phone for those who live too far away to visit.

Interacting

Caiques, especially those that are kept as single birds, need a fair amount of daily time out of their cage and human interaction. A typical caique needs to spend at least an hour a day outside of its cage and interacting with its owner. A caique out of its cage needs constant supervision—its curiosity, dexterity, and small size will often result in an unsupervised caique putting itself in mortal danger with no clue about the risks involved. Having a caique is roughly the same as having a human toddler in terms of the number of potential dangers the average household possesses, multiplied by the fact that a caique is smaller and faster than a human toddler and can disappear from sight that much more quickly.

Each bird and owner will eventually come to their own set of interactions as time goes on. Games you may enjoy playing with your caique may include toe wrestling, where the owner tries to touch the bird's feet while the bird either tries to avoid it or wrestles with the advancing finger; exploring pockets—a favorite caique sport, particularly when the owner hides a treat inside such as an almond in the shell for the bird to discover; and preening each other.

Whether or not you allow the bird to stand on your shoulder is a matter of personal choice. Some people find this a convenient way to have their caiques with them as they go about their household chores, whereas others strongly recommend against it because of the proximity of the bird's beak to the owner's vulnerable face and ears. Even the tamest bird may become startled by a sudden sound or the appearance of a stranger, and many caiques will then nip their owner in an attempt to get him or her to flee from danger.

If you decide not to allow your caique to stand on your shoulder, be very clear and consistent about it. Put your free hand across your arm to form an obstacle as soon as you realize that the bird is heading for your shoulder. If it succeeds in getting up there, remove it immediately, and if it persists, return it to its cage briefly. Training the bird to stay off your shoulder may also greatly reduce the amount of laundry you have to do in a week, because caiques can be very fast about defecating down the back of your shirt.

Preening

Preening is a particularly helpful way for an owner and caique to interact, because as new feathers grow in, they poke through the skin with all of the feather encased in a kind of pointed, waxy sheath. Caiques preen themselves, chewing on this waxy sheath to remove the casing and let the feather expand into a more aerodynamic shape. The problem for a single bird is that it can't reach the feathers on its head, neck, and face, and consequently may have a collection of unopened pinfeathers on these areas.

You may notice these prickly-looking projections when you look closely at the bird, or you may feel them if you touch the bird's head. These pinfeathers may become very uncomfortable for the bird, making it feel itchy. Very often, a caique will invite someone to help it out by preening its head and neck feathers. If you see your bird standing in front of you with its head bent low so that its forehead almost touches the floor or perch, it is asking you to help it out by preening the pinfeathers open for it.

To preen your caique, you can either scratch its head using your fingernails, much the same as you would do to a dog, or you can isolate the pinfeathers one at a time between your thumb and index finger and gently scrape off the waxy sheath with your fingernail. Be careful not to preen too close to the skin; the caique has some sensation in the pinfeathers just at the point where they erupt through the skin, and if you scratch too low, the bird may squawk and perhaps even give you a gentle tap with its beak. This isn't an aggressive act, but simply a reminder to be a little more careful. When this happens, most caiques will lower their heads again immediately, asking you to continue with your helpful ministrations.

Do not be surprised if your caique wants to return the favor by preening you. If it gently nibbles on your fingers, clothing, or hair, this is

Caiques spend much of their time preening their feathers.

exactly what it is trying to do. If the nibbling becomes too rough, simply tell the bird to be gentle, and if it doesn't comply, either try to distract it by offering it a toy to play with or move it back to its cage.

Nail Trimming

Depending on the bird's living conditions, a caique may or may not be able to keep its toenails worn down through its daily activities. Some people provide rough concrete perches to help their birds wear down their nails. A normal caique's nails should be short enough that when the bird stands with its feet on a flat surface, the entire foot lies flat. If the bird stands on a flat surface and you notice that the nails are so long that they push the toes back to the point where they are actually not in contact with the countertop or floor, then your bird's nails are too long. If your bird's nails reach the point where they dig into your skin sharply when you hold it, or they begin to catch on things as the bird moves about, then it's time to think about trimming them.

It's generally a good idea to have somebody else show you how to trim a bird's nails for the first time. This is because there's a blood vessel

Some caiques are so comfortable being handled that their owners are able to trim their nails without otherwise restraining the bird.

that runs through the center of the nail, and if you accidentally cut it along with the nail, you will cause the bird to bleed. It may be easier to trim a white-bellied caique's nails than a black-headed caique's because its nails are lighter and you may be able to see this blood vessel (called the quick) inside. Trimming the nails is also easier to do if you have two people—one to hold the bird wrapped in a towel and another to gently extend the toes and hold them in position with one hand while clipping the nails with the other. You can use a regular toenail clipper intended for people to trim your bird's nails. Remember when you are doing the actual clipping that your goal is to trim rather than shorten the nail. The trimmed nail should be just long enough for the tip to touch a flat surface when the bird stands on it. Try to cut the nail at a slight angle, so that the front edge is ever so slightly longer than the back—this helps the bird get a better grip when climbing than a flat cut allows.

If you do accidentally cut the nail too short and nick the quick so that the bird starts to bleed, remain calm. If only a drop or two is spilled, you should just leave the injured toe alone and it will clot itself. If the bird bleeds more than a couple of drops, you can either apply a styptic pencil (available at many pet stores) to stop the bleeding, or, if you don't have a styptic pencil, dip the injured nail in flour or cornstarch to promote speedy clotting.

Beak Trimming

A normal caique will keep its beak worn down to a manageable level simply through normal use. The tip of a normal caique's upper beak will reach just below the place where the lower beak meets the bird's throat. A grossly overgrown beak is a sign of a significant illness, frequently a liver problem, in which the bird's metabolism has increased to the point where the beak and nails grow faster than the bird can keep them worn down.

If you suspect that your bird's beak is overgrown, consult with an avian veterinarian. Under no circumstances should you attempt to trim it yourself. To do so is very stressful for the bird, and will not address the underlying problem. A normal, healthy caique does not need its beak trimmed.

Bathing

Caiques are natives of the rain forests of South America. For this reason, they enjoy high levels of humidity and frequent showering. Some owners don't mind sharing their own shower time with their caique. They park the bird on a nearby towel rack or on the shower curtain rod while they take their shower. When they have finished washing, they'll take the caique into the shower with them, holding it on their arms so that the water from the showerhead hits their bodies and bounces off of them spraying the caique with the resulting mist. Depending on your shower pressure, your caique may enjoy standing directly under the shower, but I usually leave that decision to the bird rather than holding it under the rushing water.

If you don't care to share your shower with your pet, you can provide it with a shallow pan of water to bathe in. A pie pan works very well for this job. I provide this option once or twice a week in the winter and more often in the summer. You may need to splash the water with your fingers or place a favorite toy in the water to encourage your bird to bathe.

A white-bellied caique.

If your caique is a reluctant bather, you can also buy a plant mister from your local garden or department store (mine came from the dollar store) and adjust the nozzle so that the water comes out in a wide, soft spray. Spray the water over the caique rather than directly at it, so that the spray falls gently on the bird from above as rain would. Most caiques enjoy getting wet, although they may not realize it the first few times it happens. Be persistent. Occasional bathing is very good for the health of their skin and feathers.

Your caique will look to you to help preen its head and neck.

Give your caique as much playful stimulus as possible.

Clipping a parrot's wings is not a permanent alteration. It involves cutting off part of the long wing feathers that a bird needs to gain altitude. When the bird molts, the cut feathers and new ones grow in to take their place, the new feathers will grow back long and intact, and the bird is once again able to take off and fly.

To clip a caique's wings, first restrain the bird in such a way that you can pull the wing away from the body without getting bitten in the process. The best way to do this is to drape a towel over the bird, being careful to cover the head as well as the body. Pick the bird up, towel and all, making sure to keep the head covered. Don't hold it too tightly—caiques need to be able to expand their chest muscles to breathe because they don't have a diaphragm the way humans do. Carefully pull the towel away from one wing, and, grabbing the wing by the bottom edge as it folds against the body, gently but firmly extend it away. Don't force the wing into an unnatural position—you don't want to break the wing bones. Simply pull the wing straight out, without pulling it up.

This is easier to accomplish if you have two people—one to restrain the bird with both hands while the other extends the wings and does the actual cutting of the feathers. However, it is possible for a single person to trim the wing feathers unassisted, using the towel to keep the bird covered and placing it on your lap so that the wing that you are not dealing with is unable to flap because it's held against your thigh.

Looking closely at the extended wing, you'll see that there are actually several rows of short feathers up near the top edge of the wing and then a row of longer feathers that skirt out from under the rows of short feathers. The wing bones actually run along the top edge of the wing. The rest of the wing is made up of feathers that have no nerves, so trimming them will not cause the bird pain. Taking a sharp pair of scissors, cut the first eight to ten of the long flight feathers about a half inch below the bottom row of short covert feathers. Release the wing, then cover the clipped side with the towel and turn the bird so that you can repeat the procedure on the opposite wing.

When you've finished clipping both wings, uncover the bird. It will probably immediately try to fly. If clipped correctly, the caique should be able to achieve some forward motion, but won't be able to

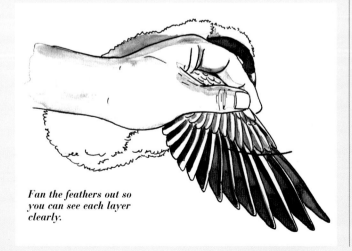

Fan the feathers out so you can see each layer clearly.

CAIQUE'S WINGS

gain any altitude. If you find that your caique is still able to take off and fly with an upward motion, try redoing the trim, cutting a little closer to the last layer of wing coverts and moving in a few more feathers' worth.

It's hard to predict exactly how long a bird will be unable to fly after a wing clipping. It depends on how long it takes the bird to molt its old feathers and grow a new set. If you trim the bird's wings just after a molt, the job will last much longer than if you do it just before it molts. For this reason, it's very important that you not take the bird outdoors, thinking that it's safe to do so because the wings are clipped. You never know when a bird will regain its ability to fly, and if the wind blows just the wrong way, it may still be able to take off, landing in a tree or on a roof where it is out of your reach.

Use the layer of feathers directly over the longest layer as a guide to where you should cut.

SAFETY

The three keys to a long and happy life for your pet are good nutrition, proper supervision to prevent accidents, and regular veterinary care. Given all three, your caique may live a long and happy life!

A Houseful of Hazards

When you let your caique out of its cage, never let it out of your sight. An unsupervised caique is sure to find trouble.

Keeping a close eye on your caique is important not only because an unsupervised bird can do irreversible damage to your belongings, but also because your house is full of potentially fatal hazards to your bird. It's impossible to completely caique-proof your house. Caiques have a habit of finding trouble that you were not even aware of, and no matter how many precautions you take, they are no replacement for supervision.

The section that follows is a room-by-room list of potential hazards, all of which could injure or kill a curious caique. The more dangers you are aware of, the safer you can make the environment for your bird.

Curious and active, caiques require a great amount of supervision when they are outside of their cages.

In the Kitchen

The kitchen is full of obvious dangers—hot stoves, sinks full of water, and electrical cords being just a few of them—but perhaps the most dangerous hazard is one that most new parrot owners aren't aware of. Most kitchens today contain at least a few pans that are covered with a nonstick coating. This coating contains a chemical called polytetrafluoroethylene or PTFE. PTFE is fairly harmless as it sits in your cabinet, but when it is heated to extremely high temperatures—536°F (282°C) or above—it begins to give off fumes that are quickly fatal to parrots.

Admittedly, this is a higher temperature than most people cook with. However, unsupervised pans may well reach this dangerous temperature, particularly if the liquid in the pan boils away to nothing or the food in the pan is allowed to burn. For this reason, caiques and other birds should not be allowed anywhere near the kitchen when nonstick cookware is in use. PTFE may also be used in hair dryers, irons, and self-

Using nonstick cookware around your caique could be life-threatening to your bird.

slips into them drowns. Electrical cords seem to be particularly tempting to caiques, who like to chew on them. A caique could easily be electrocuted by chewing on a live wire. In the case of cords that are not plugged in, be sure to visually check them if your caique has been anywhere near them, looking for any places that the wires inside the cord are exposed before plugging them in. You run the risk of fire or electrical shock if you don't.

Be careful to keep a close eye on your caique so that it doesn't inadvertently get trapped inside a cabinet, the refrigerator, or the oven, and don't venture through a door to the outside if there's a caique loose in the room. Caiques have a propensity for wanting to explore new places and may well take advantage of open doors while you are distracted by looking inside them.

In the Bathroom

Be sure to keep your bathroom cabinets and medicine chests closed, and never leave open pill bottles or loose pills out where your caique can find them. Be sure that all cleaning supplies are out of the way and out of sight lest a curious beak should want to explore them. Never leave a caique unattended when the bathtub or sink has water in it. It's too easy for a curious bird to fall in and drown. Likewise, the toilet lid as well as the seat should also be kept down when not in use, because there are reports of caiques that have actually drowned in the water in the toilet.

cleaning ovens, so you should avoid using these items when your caique is in the room.

Other kitchen hazards should be more obvious. Hot stoves run the risk of the bird landing on them and burning its feet. Sinks full of dishwater may be so deep that the bird that

Even this relaxed caique can find danger in a kitchen.

All of your belongings are fair game to a curious caique.

In the Living Room, Bedroom, and Den

Objects that are small enough for a caique's beak should be picked up and stored out of sight. This includes beaded items as well. You might not think that your pearl necklace is small enough to choke your bird, but the strings that hold them together are no match for a caique's beak, and the pearls or beads may be just the right size to choke your bird. Children's toys and games, particularly ones that have a multitude of small parts, should also be put away—both for the sake of the bird and the sake of the toys. A curious caique may have the unintended benefit of persuading your child to pick up their toys, lest they become riddled with triangular beak marks, or worse, reduced to kindling!

Your potted plants may look tempting to a curious caique. There is a partial list of safe and poisonous plants below. All plants should be kept up and (ideally) out of reach, but the

Safe Plants	Poisonous Plants
Aloe	Avocado
African Violets	Calla Lily
Coleus	English Ivy
Donkey's Tail	Hydrangea
Fir (Christmas) Tree	Larkspur
Jade Plants	Laurel
Kolanchoe	Mistletoe
Roses	Philodendron
Spider Plants	Poinsettia
Swedish Ivy	
Wandering Jew	

Because caiques love to chew, you need to be especially vigilant to protect any household item.

Top Three Things That You Didn't Know May Be Fatal to Your Caique

Nonstick cookware
Cat saliva
Avocado

smart owner will try to restrict new plant purchases to species that are known to be non-toxic. If you have your heart set on a particular plant that's on the toxic list, try to keep it in a room that's closed off to the bird, or better yet, outdoors. And even plants that are normally safe for a caique to nibble on may be poisonous if they are covered with pesticides or have plant food spilled on their leaves.

Holiday decorations should also be viewed with caution. Their bright, festive colors and interesting textures are just the thing to tempt a caique to taste them, possibly resulting in poisoning, injury, or electric shock.

Ceiling fans are also a potential danger, particularly if your caique is flighted. Even with a bird whose wings are clipped, there is always a risk that the feathers will have grown in just enough without your noticing that the bird may one day be able to take off and have a potentially fatal collision with the moving fan blades. It's always best to leave the ceiling fan off when the caique is out of its cage. Occasionally a moving ceiling fan will frighten a caique into trying to flee in terror; the overhead movement reminds them of an overhead hawk, so it's always best to leave the fan off when the bird is in the room.

Open windows and doors are always a threat, no matter what room you're in. All it takes is an unguarded moment—a child going out to play, an adult carrying groceries in, or a knock being answered—and your caique may be lost, perhaps forever. All windows should have screens in place to keep the birds indoors. The smart owner will do a "bird check" every time there's a ringing doorbell or a knock on the door to ensure that the bird is confined before the door is opened. If you share your home

Steps to Take Before Your Caique Gets Lost

✔ Take a clear, close-up picture of your bird that will be suitable to use on "Lost Bird" ads and posters.

✔ Record the information that's on the bird's leg band so that you can identify the bird as yours if it should be found.

✔ Make an audio recording of your bird when it's either playing happily or calling you.

✔ Consider having an identifying microchip implanted beneath your bird's skin by a veterinarian so that if your bird ends up at an animal shelter equipped with a microchip scanner, they can contact you.

with people who may have the bird out of its cage, you might want to consider knocking or ringing the doorbell yourself to make sure the bird is safe before the door is opened. It's also wise to look before you close any doors inside your house—you don't want to accidently squash your bird as it tries to follow you from room to room.

Birds on the Floor

A caique, particularly one whose wings are clipped, will want to get down from its cage or off of its perch to walk around on the floor of your house. And although you may find it flattering to have your bird following you from room to room as you do housework, having a bird on the floor is just an accident waiting to happen.

A bird on the floor may be inadvertently stepped on or crushed in a closing door. It is more likely to be next to an outside door when someone who doesn't know the bird is there opens it, creating an opportunity for the bird to leave the house. It is more likely to find live electrical wires to chew on, or to be injured or killed by another pet. In short, a caique that wanders around on the floor is a caique at risk.

Insist that your caique stay in or on its cage or play stand unless it is being held. Anytime the bird ventures down onto the floor, promptly return it to its perch, telling it, "You need to stay up." Hand it a toy or food treat to try to distract it from trying to get down. If it insists on trying to get back to the floor, put it back in its cage for a short "time-out," then give it another chance to be out in an appropriate location later.

Lost and Found

One of the most heartbreaking experiences that can happen to any bird owner is when a beloved, sheltered pet accidentally flies out of the house and is lost. Even a tame, friendly bird is liable to panic when suddenly faced with the unfamiliar outdoors and will follow its instinct to flee rather than return to its frantic, calling owner.

A lost bird is much easier to prevent than to recover. Avoid putting play stands and cages in sight of an outside door. At my house, the bird room is upstairs to decrease the likelihood that a bird will accidently fly out the door. Some caique owners I know keep their screen doors locked so that guests have to knock or ring the doorbell and there's a barrier still in place when they open the inner door. This is a helpful practice for the sake of the owner's safety as well.

Never take a caique out of doors unless it is in some sort of carrier. There are some harnesses

Caiques need constant supervision.

and leashes designed for birds on the market, but I don't recommend using them. They can be difficult to put on, may break the bird's feathers or rub against the skin, and may be very irritating for the caique.

There are several precautions you can take beforehand that will help in the event that your caique gets lost. Try to have a clear, close-up picture of your caique that would be suitable to use in "Lost Bird" ads and posters. If you don't have one of your bird, a generic photo of the same species of caique will do in a pinch. You can download one from the Internet.

Keep a written record of your bird's leg-band inscriptions so that you can prove that a recovered bird is yours, and keep your bill of sale or hatch certificate so that you can prove that you own the bird with that particular band number. This is particularly important if your bird is not lost but stolen. If it comes down to

a question of your claim that you are the rightful owner and the thief or recipient claiming that the bird belongs to him, this band number will prove that you are the one who rightfully owns that particular bird. You may also use the leg-band information to verify whether or not someone calling claiming to have your bird really does have it or is merely trying to scam you out of reward money. Even if they are not able to see the band to read the number, they should at least be able to tell you what color the leg band is.

Another step that you can take in advance that will help prove beyond a shadow of a doubt that your bird belongs to you is to have it microchipped. This means taking the bird to the veterinarian's and having a small microchip implanted under its skin. This chip isn't visible and doesn't seem to bother the bird once the small incision made for the insertion has healed. If the bird is found and turned over to an animal shelter that's equipped with a microchip scanner, the chip will reveal your contact information and the shelter can call you directly and reunite you with your pet. Microchipping is also more reliable than a leg band in the event that your caique is stolen. Leg bands can be removed with metal cutters. (You should never attempt to do this yourself; it's too easy to break the leg in the process. If the leg band does need to be removed, ask your veterinarian to do it.)

Another step you should take is to make an audio recording of your bird when it is either happily playing or when it is calling you. Label this recording and put it in a safe place. If your bird escapes and flies out of sight, a good first step is to set up your tape or CD player outside and play the recorded caique sounds at top volume to try to guide your caique home. If the bird can't see you, it may still be drawn to the sounds of "another" caique.

If you do lose your caique, move its cage out of doors so that it is in plain sight (not concealed under a tree or by a porch). Leave the cage doors open and the dishes stocked with food and water to tempt the bird into returning to its familiar place. Put an ad in the local newspapers describing the bird, and make posters to distribute around your neighborhood, at local grocery stores, convenience stores, bus stops—any place they might be seen. Don't merely say, "Lost Caique"—most people don't know what a caique is. Say instead, "Lost Parrot—Green back, white belly," and so forth. Don't list your bird's leg-band number, but do make sure to list your contact information. If you are able to offer a reward, say so.

Alert local veterinarians, animal shelters, animal control officers, and bird groups such as bird clubs and Audubon Society sanctuaries to be on the lookout for your bird. I also recommend placing posters near elementary schools. Children are usually very enthusiastic volunteers who have more free time than adults and are more likely to be enticed by the prospect of a reward.

If you ever find yourself in the position of having lost your pet, don't give up hope, no matter how much time your bird is gone. You never know.

Birds who are allowed out of their cage unsupervised are at a much higher risk for being lost or injured.

HEALTH

Like all parrots, caiques will do their best to appear healthy even when they are ill or injured. This is a survival strategy. In the wild, any member of the flock that appears to be less healthy than the others is more likely to be singled out by predators. For this reason, pet caiques should be seen by an avian veterinarian annually or at the first sign that something may be wrong.

Avian Veterinarians

Any veterinarian can treat a bird, but not all veterinarians are equal when it comes to treating your bird. The best veterinarians are the ones who chose to pursue a special course in avian health while they were in veterinary school, then took and passed a special test in how to treat sick and injured birds. When looking for a veterinarian for your bird, look for one that is board certified in avian medicine. You can find a certified avian veterinarian by asking the breeder, bird-owning friends, or a local bird club for a recommendation.

Not every practice that advertises the fact that it treats birds actually has a board-certified avian veterinarian working there. You have to

Towels are essential in restraining a sick or injured bird.

specifically ask if there is one, and if there is, ask to see that particular veterinarian when you make an appointment rather than one of his or her partners. Be warned, though, that avian veterinarians are not terribly common. You may have to travel quite a bit outside your hometown to find one, but it's worth the hassle to keep your bird healthy.

The New-Bird Checkup

It's always a good idea to have any new bird checked by a board-certified avian veterinarian as soon as possible. Many breeders and stores have a time limit for returning a sick bird, and if you wait, that window of opportunity may end before you realize that there's something wrong with your bird. Discovering any problems early on may also help to prevent heartache. If the bird needs to be returned to

Signs That Your Bird Needs a Veterinarian

- Steady weight loss
- Changes in droppings that cannot be attributed to dietary changes
- Sneezing, coughing, or wheezing
- Puffed feathers
- Discharge from the nostrils
- Unresponsiveness
- Unexplained vocalization, particularly when the bird is handled
- Holding a leg or wing at an unusual angle
- Changes in behavior, listlessness, or excessive sleepiness
- Changes in the feathers
- Sitting on the bottom of the cage
- Appearing to be straining as if trying to pass an egg but being unable to do so

the seller for health reasons, it's best to do it before you become emotionally attached.

A new-bird checkup will include a visual check of the bird's body. The eyes should be clear and focused. The vent area should be clean—a damp or soiled vent may indicate diarrhea. If the bird defecates in the carrier on the way to the veterinarian's, that sample should be left for the veterinarian to examine. The veterinarian will check the nostrils to make sure that they are clear and free of discharge. He or she will also look at the roof of the bird's mouth to examine papillae. Papillae are small, bumpy growths that are found in a normal, healthy bird. If these appear to be worn down, it's a sign of either chronic infection or a vitamin A deficiency.

The veterinarian may take swabs of the inside of your caique's mouth and from around the vent area to determine the levels of various bacteria present. This testing is called a Gram stain, and if your bird has an excessive amount of harmful bacteria in its system, your veterinarian will advise you about what steps to take.

The veterinarian will probably also want to draw a sample of blood to test for the presence of diseases and to determine the levels of different chemicals in the bird's system. This is important even if the bird is healthy, because it helps the veterinarian establish what is normal for your bird, so that if blood needs to be drawn at a later date because of a suspected problem, the veterinarian will have something to compare that second sample with.

If you are curious about your bird's sex, the new-bird checkup is a great time to ask the veterinarian to use some of the blood drawn for DNA testing, particularly if you want to know if your bird is a female or a male before you name it. The first visit to the veterinarian is also a good time to ask the veterinarian to show you how to trim your bird's wing feathers so that it won't be able to fly.

It is worth mentioning again that any new bird should be quarantined from any birds you already own even after the bird has been looked at by a veterinarian—both to give the veterinarian a chance to get any lab results back and in case the bird was recently exposed to any contagious conditions that haven't yet manifested themselves.

Annual Checkups

It is very important that the bird be seen by an avian veterinarian on a regular basis. In many cases, early detection of a problem may mean the difference between life and death for

Caiques are natural acrobats.

your bird. An annual checkup with a board-certified avian veterinarian is an excellent way of ensuring your bird's continued health.

Between checkups, one of the best things an owner can do to monitor a caique's health is to weigh the bird twice weekly. A postal scale or diet scale that gives the results in an LCD read-out and measures weight in grams as well as in ounces is ideal for this. Although slight fluctuations in a bird's weight are normal, a steady decline is often the first and only indication the owner may have of a serious health prob-

lem. If you notice a consistent decline in your bird's weight, consult an avian veterinarian as soon as you can.

Vaccines

There are very few vaccines available for the diseases that affect birds. One notable exception to this is the polyoma virus. Polyoma, which can be diagnosed only by a veterinarian, is almost always fatal in young parrot chicks, whereas adult birds can survive with the virus

Caiques, such as this baby black-headed chick, are outgoing from the time they are very young.

from a variety of other sources. Some people think that if a caique comes from a closed aviary and goes directly to its new home without being exposed to other birds, the vaccination is not necessary. Other people think that an ounce of prevention is worth a pound of cure and that new caiques should be vaccinated as a precaution. You should discuss the matter with your veterinarian, who will help you decide whether or not your caique should be vaccinated against the polyoma virus.

Polyoma

Polyoma is a virus that, as mentioned above, seems to affect caiques differently than other birds. Its symptoms include sudden, marked weight loss, diarrhea, shivering, and, in young birds, constant crying and a noticeable darkening of the skin covering the abdomen. Although

in their systems. However, the polyoma virus affects caiques differently, and adult caiques as well as caique chicks often succumb to it. Because the polyoma virus is transmitted from bird to bird, the vaccine is often given to caiques when they are still young, particularly if they are in a situation, such as a pet store, where they are exposed to birds that come

polyoma is preventable with a vaccine, there is no known cure once a bird contracts the virus. Once a diagnosis of polyoma has been made, it's vitally important that everything the bird has come into contact with be disinfected using a solution of one part bleach to nine parts water. If any other birds in the household might be breeding, it is important to separate them and to remove any eggs they may have rather than risk allowing the chicks to contract the virus and die a painful, inevitable death.

Proventricular Dilation Disorder

Proventricular Dilation Disorder, or PDD, is also sometimes called the wasting disease. Its cause is still unknown, although some scientists think it may be caused by a virus. PDD is a chronic condition in which the bird may either eat large amounts but steadily lose weight or stop eating, vomit, and pass undigested food in its droppings, leading to extreme weight loss. At this writing, attempts are being made to treat PDD with steroids, but there is no known cure, and the condition is always fatal.

Psittacine Beak and Feather Disease

Psittacine Beak and Feather Disease, or PBFD, is an uncurable and extremely contagious condition that is transmitted by a virus. Birds afflicted with PBFD have feathers that are broken, bent, twisted, or otherwise deformed and beaks that may be deformed. This condition is generally quickly fatal to younger birds, but older caiques can be treated with immunostimulants to help improve and prolong their lives.

Birds with PBFD should be kept in a warm place to compensate for the inadequate insulation that their deformed feathers provide. Under no circumstances should they be housed with healthy birds, and the sick bird's owner should take extreme sanitary precautions to prevent the unintentional spread of the disease. The PBFD virus can be spread by the dust from dried droppings becoming airborne or clinging to your hands or clothing. If you are unfortunate enough to have a bird with PBFD, you will need to wash your skin and change your clothes after you service or interact with your bird to avoid unwittingly spreading it to others. This is particularly important to remember if you are going to the pet store for supplies, so that you avoid accidentally infecting the store's healthy stock.

Metal Toxicity

Metal toxicity isn't a disease but a neurological condition caused when the bird accidentally ingests unhealthy amounts of toxic metals, such as lead or zinc. This results in irreversible neurological damage, which may manifest itself as seizures, impaired balance, jerky motions, or death.

Because caiques love to explore things by tasting them, caique owners need to take every step possible to ensure that their birds do not encounter any potentially toxic metals. Possible sources of toxic metal exposure can include lead or zinc soldering, particularly in antique cages, surfaces that were painted with lead-based paint that was manufactured before the dangers were known, linoleum, or some jewelry. The safest course of action is to remove any items that might contain zinc or lead from your caique's environment. If your veterinarian diagnoses a metal toxicity, it is vital that you identify the source of exposure and remove it, because the condition cannot be stabilized until you do.

Aspergillosis

Aspergillosis is a respiratory disorder caused by a fungus that takes hold in the bird's air sacs, making it difficult for the bird to breathe. It's often associated with immuno-compromised birds, an underlying illness, or an inadequate diet, such as one lacking in vitamin A. This condition is much more common in damp or unsanitary conditions, and was particularly common among imported wild-caught birds who were kept in such circumstances after they were captured. Aspergillosis is treatable in the early stages, but is much more difficult to treat if it has been allowed to progress unchecked.

Pacheco's Disease

Pacheco's disease is also known as psittacine herpes virus. Although it's usually fatal, birds that do manage to survive frequently become carriers for the virus and may infect any other birds with which they come into contact. It's very important that any bird with a diagnosis of Pacheco's disease be quarantined from other birds as soon as possible and that any birds that it may have come into contact with also be checked by a veterinarian. The bird's environment, including the cage, perches, dishes, toys, and anything else the bird might have come into contact with, should immediately be disinfected with a solution of one part bleach to nine parts hot water. A vaccine is available but may cause a negative reaction, so it is usually not given unless the bird is believed to be a carrier for the virus or may have been exposed to the virus and is at risk of contracting the disease.

Psittacosis

Psittacosis is also known as chlamydiosis or "parrot fever." It's one of the few diseases that humans can actually catch from an infected bird. It's also communicable from one bird to another and is highly contagious. Symptoms of psittacosis in caiques include the usual signs of a sick bird: unexplained weight loss, nasal discharge and/or sneezing, watery eyes, lime-green droppings, and loss of appetite. In humans, symptoms may include a high fever, fatigue, and an atypical form of pneumonia.

Psittacosis is most prevalent where the general conditions are unsanitary. A bird with psittacosis can transmit the disease when it sneezes out infected nasal discharges, or through its droppings. Psittacosis can be transmitted either through direct contact with wet droppings from an infected bird or by breathing in the dust of dried droppings that becomes airborne when the droppings are disturbed, such as when the cage is cleaned. The virus that causes the disease can remain active in the droppings and their dust for months, so the whole environment should be stringently cleaned—scrubbed, vacuumed, and disinfected—after a positive diagnosis.

Psittacosis can be diagnosed through a blood test, through a sample of the bird's droppings, or through a DNA probe, but a false negative test result may occur if the sample of droppings tested was made while the bird was not actively shedding the virus. If you or a family member are experiencing the symptoms mentioned above, you should make a point of mentioning to your health care provider that you own a parrot. Because this is not a common illness, psittacosis may not initially occur to physicians as a possible cause unless they are aware of your possible exposure to the disease. Psittacosis is easily cured by antibiotics when it's caught in the early stages.

Gram-negative Bacteria

All birds and mammals naturally have bacteria inside their digestive systems. Many of these bacteria perform useful functions, like helping break down food. Other, less helpful bacteria will also be present, but this in itself is not a health risk unless these types of bacteria begin to flourish to the point where they outnumber the helpful bacteria and start to interfere with their ability to aid the body. The number of the different types of bacteria present in a bird's digestive tract is determined by a test called a Gram stain. The helpful bacteria are called Gram-positive bacteria; the detrimental bacteria is called Gram-negative. If the Gram stain finds unacceptably high levels of Gram-negative bacteria, this is not an illness in itself but may lessen the bird's overall health, making it more susceptible to other, more harmful conditions. Your veterinarian may treat excessively high levels of Gram-negative bacteria through dietary changes, or through the use of antibiotics. Follow-up checks, to make sure that the Gram stain results return to normal levels, should be made.

Diarrhea and Polyuria

A normal caique's dropping should look like a dark green tube covered with a lace of white

An active caique that suddenly becomes very still and quiet is a sign of a possible health problem.

urates. It should be well formed and solid, not overly liquid or off-color. The exception to this is if your bird has been eating something that causes a change in its droppings. A large quantity of fruit, for example, may make the droppings more watery than usual, and certain foods, such as beets or cranberries, will change the color.

Diarrhea is when the droppings are extremely runny or watery and possibly off-color. Polyuria is an increase in the amount of urates produced by the kidneys and may also manifest itself as watery droppings. If you notice a change in your caique's droppings, review what the bird has recently had to eat and eliminate any new items or any foods that may have been in your refrigerator for a while. Eliminate these suspect causes from the bird's diet and see if the droppings return to normal. If they are still loose after 24 hours, consult your veterinarian to see if he or she can find a solution for the problem.

In the event of a significant illness, everything in the bird's environment—cages, perches, and toys—should be disinfected to avoid spreading the disease to the other birds in the house.

Mites

Mites are small insects, approximately the size of the periods on this page, that suck the blood from the birds they land on, much the same way fleas feast on the blood of cats and dogs. If your caique is scratching excessively, crying out in discomfort for no apparent reason, or pulling out its own feathers and biting at its skin, mites may be the cause.

To see if your caique is plagued with mites, replace the newspaper cage lining with plain white paper towels just before you put the bird into its cage for the night and drape the cage with a plain white cloth. In the morning, inspect the paper toweling and cloth. If you notice small red dots against the white, then you know that your bird is afflicted with mites.

There are commercial mite sprays available in many pet stores. These work well, but may require repeated applications to both the bird and the environment before the bird is completely free of the parasites. Some pet stores offer a "mite repellent" to hang on the edge of the cage, frequently including it as part of a package deal of supplies for your new bird, but you don't need this if the bird is mite-free, and it contains pesticides that may ultimately harm your caique.

Worms

There are several different types of intestinal worm that may infect your caique. Worms infest your bird's digestive system when they or their eggs or larvae are ingested. You may either observe the worms in the bird's stool or notice a sudden weight loss as the worms interfere with the bird's digestion and absorption of food. Although there are several commercial deworm-ers available, it's best to seek a veterinarian's advice to make certain you are using the most suitable medication and the most appropriate dosage. Intestinal worms are more common in caiques that are kept in outdoor aviaries with dirt floors than they are in house pets. It is not necessary to give your bird a deworming med-ication on a regular basis as a preventive. The best way to prevent worms is through good hygiene and sanitary practices.

Feather Plucking

Feather plucking is when a caique's feathers are pulled out, either by the caique itself or another bird. This should not be confused with molting, which is when the caique naturally sheds its feathers so that new ones can grow in. You may also notice that your bird will occasionally remove a feather with its beak while it preens itself, pulling it out with its beak and then dropping it onto the cage floor as part of the normal grooming process. Nei-ther of these are plucking. Feather plucking is when a multitude of feathers are removed, resulting in a very rumpled look, a bird with bald patches, or, in the extreme, a bird that is almost entirely bald.

If you notice that your caique is developing bald patches, observe carefully to see if another bird is the cause. It's normal for birds to preen each other, but once in a while you'll come across a bird that is too enthusiastic in this chore and will pluck its friend until bald

Things to Have On Hand in Case of an Emergency

✔ Carrier to transport a sick bird to the veterinarian's
✔ Eyedropper or syringe
✔ Heating pad
✔ Leg-band information
✔ Phone numbers for your veterinarian and the Animal Poison Control hotline (888) 462-4435
✔ Styptic pencil
✔ Tweezers

patches begin to appear. If this is the case, try to keep the birds separate for a while to give the feathers a chance to grow back in and then monitor them closely in the future, limiting their time together to avoid excessive preening. If you do this, you may want to make a point of scratching your caique's head for it, since it can't reach the pinfeathers on its head and they are liable to be itchy as they grow back in.

A caique who plucks his own feathers to the point of baldness presents a much greater prob-lem. There can be several causes, and it can be very difficult to determine why the bird has developed this behavior. The first step would be to take the bird to an avian veterinarian to find out if it has a physiological condition. Plucking can be caused by poor nutrition, mites, stress, boredom, or disease. Determining the cause is the first step in finding a cure.

Feather plucking caused by a psychological condition is much harder to stop than behavior that has a physiological cause. Caiques may pluck out of boredom, which can be alleviated through the introduction of new toys and increased owner interaction. They may pluck if they are anxious about their surroundings, so you may wish to be particularly observant about how the rest of the household—including other pets and children—interact with the bird and whether or not the bird is witnessing a stressful event. One person I know could not figure out why her bird would suddenly start screaming and thrashing in the middle of the day, until she realized that a hawk was raiding her backyard bird feeder. She had positioned the cage so that her caique had a clear view of the bird feeder, thinking that it would enjoy seeing the wild birds. The stress of seeing other birds killed and eaten made her caique very anxious. She moved the cage, but it was quite a while before her caique finally seemed to relax and not start at sudden movements.

Chronic Egg Laying

This is not an extremely common problem with caiques, but it does occasionally occur. If you have a male caique, you will never have to worry about this, and if you have a female caique, you may still never see an egg. But, as with all birds, there may be times when a female caique lays an egg. This ordinarily is not a problem. She may want to sit on the egg and go through the motions of roosting, and may be very protective of it and very aggressive toward anyone who approaches it. Unless the aggression reaches an intolerable level, it's best to let her sit on the egg for as long as she wants to. Eventually—and this may take several weeks—she will lose interest and stop sitting, at which time you will be able to remove and dispose of it. If you remove the eggs promptly and don't let her sit on them, this may cause her to lay "replacement" eggs, creating a real

strain on her body and using up her calcium reserves as she produces more eggs than she would if she were allowed to keep them.

Every now and then, there'll be a hen whose hormones run a bit amok, and she will lay more eggs more frequently than is normal. If your bird lays eggs more often than once every six months, then she is laying excessively. If this is the case, you can do several things to discourage her from laying. Cover the cage earlier in the evening and uncover it later in the morning so that the bird has fewer hours of exposure to daylight. This may fool the bird into thinking that winter—the season in which they don't ordinarily lay their eggs—is approaching. You can also try moving her cage every few days to keep her feeling just a bit unsettled so that she won't be comfortable enough to lay eggs. In an extreme case, you may need to consult with an avian veterinarian to find a medical solution.

Blood Feathers

When feathers first break through the skin, they contain blood vessels that reach up into the shaft of the feather. This blood supply diminishes and eventually ceases as the feather grows. If you look closely, you may recognize this blood supply in emerging feather shafts by a dark blue-purple color inside the shaft close to the skin. Ordinarily this blood supply doesn't pose a problem, but if the feather is cut or broken, the shaft may start to bleed. Sometimes the broken blood feather will clot and cease to bleed on its own, but there are times when the broken shaft will bleed unchecked. If this is the case, then it's necessary for the owner to stop the bleeding by pulling out the broken feather.

To remove a bleeding blood feather, restrain the bird with a towel, covering its head to keep it from interfering with the procedure. Isolate the broken shaft, grasping it firmly just above the skin, using tweezers or pliers. If you are not too squeamish, you may use your fingers instead, as long as you wash your hands first. Pull the shaft up and out in the direction that the feather grows in, using one firm, sharp pull. Removing this broken shaft will cause the caique to feel a slight pain, much the same as you would feel if someone were to pluck out one of the hairs on your head, so don't be alarmed if the bird flinches and squawks when you pull the offending feather out. If there's any residual bleeding after you remove the shaft, you can stop it by using a styptic pencil or applying cornstarch to encourage the wound to clot.

A caique that is used to being handled is generally easier to manage at the veterinarian's office.

Egg Binding

Most caiques can pass an egg without a problem. On rare occasions, however, either a hen will be too small or an egg will be too large for it to pass out of the bird's body. If this is the case, you may notice the bird squatting on the bottom of the cage, straining as if trying to push something out of her body. If you look at the bird's cloaca, you may notice that it's swollen and gaping, and you may actually be able to see the white eggshell lurking just inside. As much as the hen strains, she is unable to expel the egg from her body. This condition is called egg binding, and it can be an extremely urgent situation. Left unchecked, it can result in the hen's death.

If you suspect egg binding, consider it a life-threatening emergency. Contact your avian veterinarian immediately for advice. If you are unable to reach your veterinarian, try placing the hen on a heating pad to help the muscles relax. Try to rub warm (not hot) olive oil or vegetable oil on the bird's vent to help lubricate the egg's passage into the world. Don't try to break the egg inside the bird—in doing so, you may accidently puncture the bird's cloaca, or the bird may be lacerated by sharp bits of broken shell.

You should trim your caique's wings just after a molt. This way, the job will last much longer.

A black-headed caique at 10 weeks.

There may be times when, for whatever reason, your veterinarian prescribes an oral medication for your caique. Medicating a caique can be a bit tricky. You can't just put the medication in their drinking water and expect that they'll get a proper dosage that way. For one thing, you cannot control how much of the medication a bird ingests if it is added to the water supply. For another, the water is much more likely to become a breeding ground for potentially harmful bacteria once foreign substances are added to it.

If your veterinarian prescribes an oral medication, it will usually be in a liquid form. He or she will provide you with a needle-less syringe as well as the medication before you leave the office. This syringe will have graduated measurements on the side to allow you to fill it with precisely the right amount of medication. To measure out the medication, push the plunger of the syringe completely down, then put the tip end into the bottle of medication. Slowly pull back the plunger to draw the medication into the barrel of the syringe. Watch carefully so that you can stop when the amount of medication reaches the correct measurement that is printed on the side of the barrel. Turn the tip point up. If there's any air in the barrel, you can carefully push the plunger to expel the extra air, stopping when the medication is exactly at the mouth of the tip.

It's generally a good idea to draw the medication into the syringe before you go to restrain the caique. It's not easy to draw the medication in the syringe one-handed while holding a struggling bird. The actual giving of the medication is not unlike the way you would hand-feed a baby bird. If possible, have one person hold the bird while you give the medication, but it is possible for a single person to both restrain and medicate the caique if necessary.

The best way to restrain a caique while you medicate it is to wrap its body in a towel. Drape the towel over the bird's back and then wrap it around the body, leaving the head exposed. Hold the bird carefully, keeping the wings pinned to its body with your hands.

I've never found that I needed to do anything to get the bird to open its mouth to squirt the medicine into it. Caiques generally don't appreciate being restrained and will bite at the restraining towel and whatever else they can reach in an effort to free

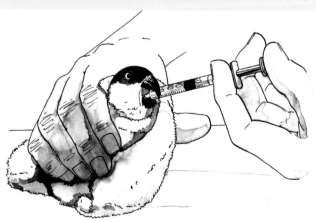

Be careful to point the syringe from right to left.

themselves. If you can manage it, try to hold the bird's head from around the back with your left hand so that it can't move it. Holding the syringe in your right hand, bring the tip to the bird's mouth. Put the syringe in the beak from the right-hand side as the bird is facing you, and depress the plunger. Administering the medication quickly gives the bird less of a chance to jerk its head free, making you spill the medication rather than getting it into the bird.

Squirting the medication in from the right side and aiming the tip of the syringe toward the left will help to ensure that it goes to the caique's stomach rather than to its lungs. Your caique will generally not be happy with you when you release it from the towel. I generally try to give mine a treat after medicating them—either a food treat to help them get the taste out of their mouths or a shower to help them get their minds off their ordeal.

It's generally a good idea to keep a sick or injured caique in a makeshift infirmary rather than returning it to its regular cage, particularly if it shares its cage with another bird. An infirmary is a small, solid-sided enclosure that can be used to keep the bird warm. Warmth will help to keep an injured bird from going into shock, and will allow a sick bird to devote its energy to getting well rather than having to maintain its body temperature.

An infirmary cage can be made from an aquarium or a small, plastic reptile cage. Use a new container for this purpose rather than one that previously housed a reptile or some other critter. The sides of the container should be clear so that you can see the patient, and solid so that drafts are kept out and the bird is unable to climb up the sides and risk further injury.

A treat is a great reward for being a good bird.

The cage should be lined with newspapers or soft cloth. Terry cloth towels, with their loops of material, should not be used because the caique's toenails can get caught in the loops. Low dishes for food and water should be placed in the narrow end of the cage, against the wall so that they are less likely to be walked on and spilled.

Heating pads or electric blankets should be used externally to keep the cage warm. They should be placed against or wrapped around one end of the infirmary, or one side of the infirmary container should be placed on top of the heat source. It's important to make sure that the source of heat doesn't encompass the entire infirmary so that the caique has a cooler section of the container to move to in the event that it feels uncomfortable.

The ideal temperature for a makeshift infirmary is between 85 and 90°F. Never put an old-fashioned mercury thermometer inside the infirmary to monitor the temperature. The glass tube of the thermometer is no match for a caique beak and the mercury inside is toxic to the caique, to you, and to the environment.

SPECIAL CAIQUE BEHAVIOR

Everyone knows that a dog will wag its tail when it's happy and growl when it wants to show aggression. Parrots have similar ways of expressing themselves. Owners who can interpret their caiques' body language will have happier, more interactive relationships with their pets.

Parrots are famous for their ability to communicate with us in our own language, and most owners eventually learn to interpret the sounds that their caiques make as well, being able to distinguish the difference between a happy chirp, a "Come here" beeping, and a playful growl. Less obvious and perhaps harder to interpret is the caique's body language.

A smart owner will learn to read the caique's body language and use that as a guide for how to interact with it. Recognizing when a caique is angry or tired will help the owner avoid being bitten by a bird who was simply not in the mood to interact.

A black-headed caique.

Beak Grinding

A caique that sits on its perch or ventures into its sleeping place may start making a strange, rumbly noise. When the owner looks closely, he or she may notice that the bird is actually grinding its beak by making small chewing motions even though there is no food in its mouth. This is a sign of a tired, contented parrot who is likely to fall asleep shortly. Caiques frequently sleep with their heads turned around so that their "chins" rest on their backs. If you hear your bird grinding its beak and notice it sitting with its head turned around, it's best to let it go to sleep undisturbed. After all, you don't like to be bothered when you're trying to settle down to sleep, do you?

A caique will keep its beak trimmed with constant use.

Tail Wagging

A caique that sits up straight on its perch and waggles its tail in a rapid blur is telling you that he is awake, alert, and happy. This behavior is often seen in a bird who wants to play.

Body Rubbing and Hair Surfing

Caiques in the wild will rub their bodies against the broad, wet leaves of the jungle.

Exactly why they do it isn't certain—they may be bathing themselves in the dew that sits on the leaves, or they may simply do it because they like the feeling. In captivity, caiques often rub their bodies against whatever is handy. One of their favorite things to rub against is their owner's hair or body.

Most caiques seem to love "hair surfing" and "body surfing," but these can quickly become tiresome for the owner. If you have a bird that wants to do this, but you would rather not have your pet playing in your hair, gently remove the bird from your person and set it down on its play stand or in its cage. Be prepared to offer the caique a toy as a distraction, because once a caique begins this activity, it really doesn't want to stop.

Feather Puffing

A caique who stands or sits with its feathers puffed up is sending an important message, but this behavior needs to be looked at in context to determine exactly what that message is.

A caique that sits on the bottom of its cage with its feathers puffed, unmoving, with its eyes either closed or half closed, may be in serious trouble. These are all signs of a sick bird. Because birds hide their illnesses for as long as possible, you can assume that by the time the bird is lying on the cage floor, it is seriously ill. The feathers may be puffed out in an effort to regulate the body temperature. If you see a bird in this position, do not hesitate—get the bird to an avian veterinarian as soon as possible.

Caiques may also puff their feathers out from their bodies if the room temperature is making them uncomfortable; it's a way of trying to cool off. The bird may also hold its wings slightly away from its body in an effort to bring its temperature down. If you notice your bird doing this on a hot day, move it to a more comfortable location. A nice shower may also be appreciated.

The last reason a caique may sit with its feathers puffed out is to show aggression. This is usually accompanied by an unrelenting glare and possibly a snapping beak. If you notice your caique puffed and staring, it's best to steer clear of it until the mood passes. Mood swings are particularly common in parrots who are experiencing fluctuations in their hormone levels. If this is the case, the bird will likely return to normal in a few days. If you see a bird that puffs and glares consistently every time you approach it, you may want to have it checked by a veterinarian. If the bird has an injury such as a broken bone, it may be trying to physically warn you off rather than risk being inadvertently hurt when you pick it up.

Head Bobbing

A caique that nods its head vigorously, possibly with its mouth open, when you come into the room is a bird that is very happy to see you. Birds that want to woo another bird in the wild will court their intended by feeding it. Because birds have no hands to carry or pass food, they do this the same way they would feed their young—by ingesting the food and then regurgitating it into the recipient's mouth. For the most part, your caique will content itself with going through the motions of regurgitating for you, but every now and then there is a caique who is not content to just go through the motions and will actually produce prechewed food for you.

If no one is available to scratch their heads for them, caiques will rub up against toys or other objects to get the job done.

If you are "lucky" enough to have a bird who regurgitates for you, try to accept this "gift" in the spirit in which it was intended. Your bird likes you and is trying to feed you. Like the cat who proudly presents an owner with a mouse, the caique expects you to understand and appreciate the effort that it went to on your behalf. Thank the bird in the cheeriest voice you can muster, then clean up the debris. As a general rule, this is not an ongoing behavior—it will occur less and less frequently and then stop altogether, presumably when the bird decides that it has won your affections.

Regurgitating should not be confused with vomiting. When a bird regurgitates, only a

Caiques express their affection by regurgitating food to feed to their loved one.

small quantity of food is produced—perhaps a beakful—and the food will look more or less like it did when the bird swallowed it. It will look chewed, but it won't look digested or discolored, or be accompanied by fluids. A bird that is vomiting will produce larger amounts and won't be able to control its body's rejection of its stomach contents. If your bird is vomiting, get it to an avian veterinarian as soon as possible, as it may have ingested something poisonous and its very life may be in danger.

Blinking

When a wild caique is being stalked, the predator will stalk the bird slowly, staring at the bird as it approaches to avoid losing track of it. To break visual contact by blinking assures the bird that you are not hunting it. In most cases, if you blink at a caique, the caique will blink back at you as a way of reassuring you that it perceives no threat. Blinking slowly and deliberately is kind of a nonverbal "I'm okay; you're okay" for parrots. This is also a useful way of reassuring an anxious bird. Although caiques are not as easily upset as, say, African greys, a caique that's upset may be reassured by your talking softly and blinking frequently at it.

Head Bowing

You may notice your caique standing with its forehead low to the ground, almost like it's

Caiques love to have their heads and necks rubbed and scratched and will lower their heads to invite you to accommodate them.

bowing to you. This is your caique's way of asking you to help it out by scratching the back and sides of its head and neck, places that it cannot preen itself. For more on preening, see the section called "Maintaining Your Caique." Some caiques will also encourage you to preen them by preening you first, gently nibbling on your finger from hand to tip so that it ends with your fingertip right on its head or face or neck, hoping that you will take the hint and give it a nice scratching in the places it can't reach.

Rubbing Its Bottom

People tend to forget that their pets have a sexual side. Because birds are generally not spayed or neutered like dogs and cats, they experience changes in their hormone levels and all of the urges and mood swings that can go with it. A bird, either a male or female, that is experiencing sexual urges but has no access to a suitable mate may try to relieve some of its sexual frustration by rubbing its vent area against a perch or some other object—in a word, masturbating. This is fairly normal behavior for a bird who is sexually frustrated, and does not mean that it is deviant or that you have to go out and purchase a prospective mate.

So if you notice your bird pressing its bottom against a perch or other hard object with its tail swishing back and forth like a demented pendulum, just look the other way and wait until it's finished. The bird would not appreciate being interrupted.

Stretching

Birds stretch for the same reason people do—to get their circulation moving after a rest or simply because it feels good. A stretching caique is one who is getting ready for another round of playing. If you see your caique stretching, it's probably a good time for you to begin interacting with your bird.

Standing on One Foot

Parrots spend most of their lives on their feet, even sleeping standing up. As you might expect, their feet sometimes become tired, and the bird will pull one of them close to its body,

rally, an occasional one-footed stance is not anything to worry about.

"Getting Tall"

A caique who encounters a new circumstance or sees something that it perceives as a potential danger will attempt to make itself as difficult to see as possible. This is achieved by pulling the wings into the body and stretching the head up toward the sky to make itself as thin as possible, and then remaining very still until the perceived threat is over. A caique who assumes this stance is best not handled, and the owner should try to remove or obscure whatever he or she thinks might be causing this reaction.

Beak Wiping

There are essentially two reasons that a caique will wipe its beak against a solid surface. The first is to clean off its beak. Caiques are notoriously messy eaters, but they don't like the feeling of sticky foods clinging to their beaks, and will rub them against the nearest convenient surface—a perch, the side of their dish, even against you if you happen to be holding it at the time!

A caique will also wipe or tap its beak vigorously against its perch or another surface if it's feeling frustrated. The precise reason for the frustration may be that the bird wants your attention and isn't getting it, or there may be some other reason that's not apparent to you. Try talking to the bird in a pleasant tone of voice and see if that persuades it to stop the motion. If it doesn't, I would advise approaching a beak-wiping caique with a bit of caution, lest it decide to take its frustration out on you!

An alarmed caique will try to make itself as tall and thin as possible.

curling the claws into something resembling a fist. This is normal. As long as your caique puts weight on its foot when it's not tucked in close to the body and walks and hops about natu-

A healthy, well-socialized caique can make a wonderful, long-term companion.

Playtime for these happy pets.

INFORMATION

Resources

Association of Avian Veterinarians
P.O. Box 811720
Boca Raton, FL 22481-1720
(561) 393-8901
http://www.aav.org

Pet Poison Control Hotline
(888) 462-4435
(A fee will be charged for this call, but it's
a great resource if you suspect your bird has
been poisoned and you can't reach your
veterinarian.)

Magazines

Bird Talk
P.O. Box 57347
Boulder, CO 80322
http://www.animalnetwork.com/birdtalk

Bird Times
Pet Publishing, Inc.
7-L Dundas Circle
Greensboro, NC 27407
http://www.petpublishing.com/birdtimes/

Companion Parrot Quarterly
PBIC Inc.
P.O. Box 2428
Alameda, CA 94501-0254
http://www.companionparrot.com

Books

Athan, Mattie Sue. *Guide to a Well-Behaved
Parrot.* Hauppauge, NY: Barron's Educational
Series, Inc., 1993.
Blanchard, Sally. *Companion Parrot Handbook.*
Alameda, CA: Pet Bird Report, 1999.
McWaters, Alicia. *A Guide to a Naturally
Healthy Bird: Nutrition, Feeding, and Natural
Healthy Methods for Parrots.* Sheffield, MA:
New Century Publishing, 1997.

*Caiques love
the water.*

Dedication

To my grandmother, Mary E. Gorman, from whom I not only got my name but also my love of animals. This one is for you, Nana.

Acknowledgments

The author wishes to thank the following people for their assistance in the preparation of this manuscript: Bob and Ginny Queen of Queens Pride Aviary in Kendalia, Texas; Jack Gilad and Doug Hauer and Gromit; Edna Bresnahan and the staff of The Crystal Parrot in Southampton, MA; the participants in the Up at Six online caique chat; the Bertrand Family; Katie Fox; and Beth Gorman.

About the Author

Mary Gorman has been raising and caring for exotic birds, including caiques, since 1982. A freelance writer in western Massachusetts, her writing includes articles in *Ranger Rick; Bird Talk; Bird Times; Original Flying Machine;* and *Companion Parrot Quarterly* magazines, as well as Barron's *Lovebirds.* She holds an M.A. from the University of Massachusetts in Amherst, and currently lives with her two children, assorted birds, and one exceedingly patient cat.

Important Note

This book deals with the care and maintenance of caiques. People who are allergic to feathers or feather dust should not keep birds. If you are not sure whether you might have such a bird allergy, consult a doctor before buying birds.

When birds are handled, they sometimes bite and scratch. Have such wounds immediately treated by a physician.

Although psittacosis is not common among caiques, it can produce symptoms in both humans and birds and can be very serious. If you have any reason to suspect psittacosis, and have flu or cold symptoms, see a doctor immediately.

Cover Photos

Bucsis & Somerville: Front and Back covers, Inside Back cover and Inside Front cover.

Photo Credits

DJ Feathers Aviary: pages 5, 8, 11 (top), 12, 14, 17, 19, 21, 27, 30, 42, 43, 45, 51, 56, 57, 61, 67, 71, 72, 80, 81, 85, 91, 92, 93; Bucsis & Somerville: pages 6, 9, 11 (bottom), 15, 16, 20, 24, 29, 31, 36, 37, 39, 40, 47, 48, 49, 50, 60, 62, 66, 69, 75, 84, 87, 96; Mary Gorman: pages 2–3, 7, 25, 32, 41, 55, 79, 88, 90; Jack Gilad and Doug Hauer: pages 10, 33, 34, 35; Sergei Vaillancourt: pages 4, 28, 53, 54, 63, 64, 68, 76, 86, 89.

All inquiries should be addressed to:
Barron's Educational Series, Inc.
250 Wireless Boulevard
Hauppauge, NY 11788
www.barronseduc.com

ISBN-13: 978-0-7641-3446-3
ISBN-10: 0-7641-3446-9

Library of Congress Catalog Card No. 2005054552

Library of Congress Cataloging-in-Publication Data
Gorman, Mary.
Caiques / Mary Gorman.
p. cm. — (Complete pet owner's manual)
Includes index.
ISBN-13: 978-0-7641-3446-3
ISBN-10: 0-7641-3446-9
1. Caiques (Birds) I. Title. II. Series.

SF473.P3G67   2006
636.6'865—dc22   2005054552

Printed in China
9 8 7 6 5 4 3 2 1